D0861204

My Heart Flooded With Water

Selected Poems
by Alfonsina Storni

My Heart Flooded With Water

Selected Poems by Alfonsina Storni

Translated
by
Orlando Ricardo Menes

Latin American Literary Review Press
Pittsburgh, Pennsylvania

Acknowledgements:

This publication is made possible in part by support
from the Institute for Scholarship in the Liberal Arts,
College of Arts and Letters, University of Notre Dame.

This project was also supported by the Pennsylvania Council on the Arts,
a state agency, through its regional arts funding partnership,
Pennsylvania Partners in the Arts (PPA).
State government funding comes through an annual appropriation
by Pennsylvania's General Assembly.
PPA is administered in Allegheny County
by Greater Pittsburgh Arts Council.

PENNSYLVANIA
COUNCIL
ON THE
ARTS

Library of Congress Cataloging-in-Publication Data

Storni, Alfonsina, 1892-1938.
[Poems. English. Selections]
My heart flooded with water: selected poems / by Alfonsina Storni;
translated by Orlando Ricardo Menes.
    p. cm.
Includes bibliographical references.
I. Menes, Orlando Ricardo. II. Title.
PQ7797.S74A2 2009
861'.62--dc22

                                                                    2009029398

Acknowledgments

I am grateful to those publications where these translations first appeared, sometimes in earlier forms and with different titles:

American Poetry Review: "Autumn," "Storm and Men," and "Prophecy."

International Poetry Review: "Portrait of García Lorca."

The Literary Review: "América's Sun."

The Malahat Review: "Buenos Aires Danzón," "Baroque Self-Portrait," and "River Plate in the Rain."

Mid-American Review: "Men in the City," "Sadness," "Twilight," "Sundays," "Silent March," "The 20th Century," and "The Word."

New England Review: "Lighthouse in the Night," "Toad and Sea," "Fog," "Street," and "Lines to the Sadness of Buenos Aires."

Southern Humanities Review: "Clouds and Sails. "

Seneca Review: "Portrait of a Boy Named Siegfried," "Two Words," "Beach," "Gray Morning," "The Hunter of Landscapes," "Plea to Prometheus," "To Eros," and "Siren."

Sycamore Review: "Drizzle," "City Jungles," "I Live on the Sea Floor," and "The World Is Sour."

Tampa Review: "Tropics."

for my wife Ivis and our two children,
Valerie and Adrian

Table of Contents

Introduction

Although relatively unknown to readers in the United States, the Argentine Alfonsina Storni (1892-1938) is one of the preeminent voices in Latin American poetry of the twentieth century, and among women poets, second only, perhaps, to the Nobel laureate Gabriela Mistral. Gwen Kirkpatrick, writing in Gale's *Modern Spanish American Poets*, states that "Storni has become a legend, not just in Argentina but also in the Spanish-speaking world.... She was truly a pathfinder for women in literature" (344). Ever since her death 70 years ago, multiple editions of her selected poetry (*antologías*) have been published in Spain and in Latin America, and even individual volumes, such as *Languidez/Languor* (1920), continued to sell well into the 1990's. And though Storni's fame rests on her poetry, she also wrote voluminously in other genres, including literary essays, autobiographical sketches, travel accounts, short stories, two novels, as well as plays for children and adults.

Storni was born on May 29, 1892, in Sala Capriasca, Ticino Canton, Switzerland, to Italian Swiss parents who had lived in Argentina for some years, and in 1896 she and her family returned to that country, settling first in the provincial city of San Juan and later that of Rosario. Though the Stornis were prosperous and socially prominent, their fortunes deteriorated in 1904 when they were forced to close their restaurant Café Suizo because of a downturn in Argentina's economy. Depressed over the family's misfortune, her father began to drink heavily and refused to look for work, abandoning the family for days while on hunting trips. Two years later he died prematurely from alcoholism. This ineffectual father becomes the haunting and burdensome figure in "Peso ancestral" (Ancestral Weight) from her third volume *Irremediablemente* (Irremediably), published in 1919. During this impecunious period when they moved to a humbler home, eleven-year-old Storni and her mother supported the household by sewing, and by age twelve she even managed to pay the rent on her own. At fourteen she was working in a factory making caps. This precipitous descent from relative affluence to poverty must have been a harrowing, though formative, experience for the young Storni, who quickly steeled herself and learned the importance of hard work, perseverance, and independence; indeed, her prose and dramatic writings would reflect a lifelong preoccupation with feminist and class themes. According to her principal biographers, writing and performing were at this time embarrassingly private and secretive, as with perhaps all young girls, and, in fact, at age twelve she began to write her first poems, sometimes stealing forms from the post office for lack of paper (Delgado 34). Her idiosyncratic nature was already revealing itself too. Biographers Silvia Galán and Graciela Gliemmo note that she despised dolls (29) and was already fascinated with death, her own and that of others (45, 48).

In 1907 Storni left her home to join a theater company, touring throughout Argentina until she returned home in 1909 to enroll at a normal school in nearby Coronda with just a second-grade education to her credit (Galán and Gliemmo 45). She received the title of "Maestra Rural" in 1910, and then began to teach elementary school in Rosario the following year. However, that job lasted just a few months when she was forced to resign for getting pregnant out of wedlock, and she moved to Buenos Aires with hardly any clothes and a few books of the poet Rubén Darío in her suitcase (Delgado 45). In 1912, a month before turning twenty, Storni gave birth to Alejandro, her one and only son. Little is known about the father, except that he was an older married man who had a prominent social position in Rosario (Galán and Gliemmo 56). Between the years 1912 and 1916, Storni struggled to make a living in a man's world, first working as a cashier, then as a salesperson, and finally as a market researcher, all three jobs that she simply found dreadful. At this time she began to contribute poetry and journalistic pieces to various periodicals, including the socialist *Proteo* and the women's magazine *El Hogar*. Then in 1916 she published her first collection, entitled *La inquietud del rosal* (Restlessness of the Rosebush), characterized by sexual candor, transgressive humor, and a defiance of the patriarchy. Storni had shed the veil of feminine modesty and spoken with *atrevimiento* (temerity) about the internal life of a woman, thereby causing a scandal. As Galán and Gliemmo point out, contemporary male critics were shocked by "the frankness of 'Miss Alfonsina Storni' who, contrary to the social customs of the time followed by a majority of women, dares to speak and publicly express her desires, her feelings, and her ideas" (86).[1] Although Storni maintained later in her career that *La inquietud del rosal* proved a fortuitous debut, opening doors wide to the literary world and to subsequent fame, she judged the book to be a work of rank amateurism destined for the flame (Galán and Gliemmo 92). No wonder then that this first book was absent from her *Selected Poems* (Antología poética), published in the year of her death.

Should we accept Storni's harsh self-criticism as the ultimate word? Yes, it is true that *La inquietud del rosal* shows derivative influences of the Romantic Gustavo Adolfo Bécquer and the *modernista* Rubén Darío.

Just as in the poetry of Bécquer, subjectivity displays a tendency toward cloyingness, the voice toward naïveté, and emotion is all too easily projected onto nature. Style also reflects the *modernista* impulse toward refined diction and rarefied symbolism.[2] Nonetheless, as the critic Sonia Jones points out, Storni is "criticized by many Modernists [*modernistas*]... for failing to write poetry whose primary goal was to create 'art for art's sake'" (52). This idea is central to the *modernista* aesthetic, just as it is central to that of the Parnassian poets. While Storni at this time had certainly read the poetry of Darío and even that of Paul Verlaine and Charles Baudelaire (read her sobering indictment of the latter in "Femenina"/"Female" from *Ocre/Ocher*), she was not, and would never be, an ideological follower of any school or movement. Indeed, Jones argues that the "influence [of *modernismo*] on her poetry was only superficial... [for she] went on her own way and created her own aesthetic ideal, which she once described as 'an attempt to mix art and life, and to learn to scorn death while still of sound mind, body, and spirit'" (53). For example, the exclamation "¡Triunfe el óvulo" (Victory to the ovule!) from her poem "Fecundidad" (Fruitfulness) suggests a quirky feminism that is more indicative of an idiosyncratic and highly personal voice than a schooled adherence to any poetics. As Jones explains, Storni "was interested in studying the goals put forward by the various artistic schools both inside and outside Argentina, but her approach was eclectic" (51).

From the start of her literary career, Storni raised eyebrows for her controversial feminism, her indomitable honesty, and her barbed wit, these being traits that in a society ruled by men would surely have brought censure, if not ostracism, to a more ordinary woman, one not so blessed with dogged independence, prodigious production, and exorbitant talent. Indeed, she took on the role of *enfant terrible* with gusto, displaying a gleeful propensity for mockery and impish behavior. In fact, her Chilean contemporary Gabriela Mistral, who would win the Nobel prize in 1945, expressed consternation over Storni's demeanor in their correspondence, as quoted in Galán and Gliemmo's *La otra Alfonsina*: "Alfonsina has shown herself to be 'selfish, mocking, and at times willfully banal'" (15).[3] Storni herself acknowledged that this unconventional nature had proven a hindrance to her literary career, specifically with those in positions of authority who doled out sinecures usually reserved for more acquiescent writers: "I have always lived, and I shall continue to live, like a feather in the breeze, with no shelter of any kind. This is very bad in an environment which judges everything by appearances. Here, when a person is being considered for some restful and important position, such as the kind that are given to writers so that they can dedicate themselves to their work, nobody asks whether that person is likely to produce something of value but rather whether he is good at living according to social formalities" (qtd. in Jones 45).

Since arriving at Buenos Aires in 1912, Storni had worked tirelessly to create a literary life while at the same time providing for her son. She thus spent long hours at work and equally long hours at home writing poetry, articles, and fiction. As an artist worn down by the incessant (and conflicting) demands of the office world, Storni suffered exhaustion, anxiety, and even depression. Her life took a dramatic turn in 1917 when the owners of Freixas y Compañía, unhappy that she was the author of *La inquietud del rosal*, gave her an ultimatum: either stop writing "scandalous" poetry and we will give you more money and benefits, or be fired. To their dismay, Storni promptly resigned and returned to teaching, which resulted in a substantial loss in pay but more time to build a writing career. As someone always savvy to the business of poetry, Storni gave frequent readings throughout Buenos Aires and across the River Plate in Montevideo, Uruguay, including the library of the Socialist Party, where this former actress mesmerized audiences with her stage presence. She began to contribute poems and articles to notable magazines and newspapers, among them *Caras y Caretas* and *La Nación*, as well as promoted her first book at the various cafes where *tertulias* (literary salons) were held, and in this exciting world of artists, she made long-lasting friends who, impressed with her passionate personality, praised Storni as "an authentic poet" (Delgado 56). These friends included the Uruguayan poets Juana de Ibarbourou and Delmira Agustini, whom Storni "considered to be the greatest poet of Latin America" (Jones 40). When the latter was murdered by her jealous husband, Storni wrote "Palabras para Delmira Agustini" (Words for Delmira Agustini), one of her most moving elegies. Between the years 1918 and 1920, her poetic output was astonishing, with no less than three collections published in quick succession: 1918's *El dulce daño* (The Sweet Hurt), 1919's *Irremediablemente* (Irremediably), and 1920's *Languidez* (Languor). While these were years of veritable success, many women, however, initially rejected her poetry as immoral because of the combative, sexually assertive feminism found in lines like "I have a son, fruit of love, lawless love" from her poem "La loba" (She-Wolf).

By the early 1920's Storni's fame had grown in the River Plate region as she gave conferences, organized poetry festivals, and won coveted awards, including the Primer Premio Municipal and the more prestigious Segundo Premio Nacional de Literatura. Storni's poetry became more ambitious formally, and her feminist ideology more articulate (as in "Tú me quieres blanca" [You Wish I Were Fair] and the more famous "Hombre pequeñito" [Little Man].) In volumes like *Languidez* and *Ocre* (1925), the predominant personae are those of women—independent, sensual—trapped in a male-dominated society that seeks to suppress their sexuality, driving them to depression and despair. In fact, *Ocre* was immensely popular, numbering three printings and one translation into French. However, the prose poems of *Poemas de amor* (Love Poems), published a year later, were uncharacteristically earnest, to the point of naivete, as well as loose in structure. The collection was received coldly by critics, despite being a commercial success.

And though erotic enjoyment is central to her feminism, she questioned whether men could offer anything more than ephemeral pleasure (Delgado 114). Storni herself was sexually liberated and sometimes even extravagant in her speech. Nevertheless, her artistic friendship with the eccentric Uruguayan writer Horacio Quiroga was, according to Josefina Delgado, a love affair that they maintained with unusual discretion for almost twenty years. Storni included no facts at all about their relationship in her papers (Delgado 84). She did not shy away, however, from expressing her captivation for the man as an artist: "Horacio Quiroga belongs to the group of instinctive geniuses, of writers unequaled, arbitrary, unilateral, and individualistic" (qtd. in Delgado 87).[4] The elegy "A Horacio Quiroga" (To Horacio Quiroga), written in 1937, pays homage to this iconoclastic man in language that is unusually direct and intimate.

By the late 1920's and early 1930's Storni was undoubtedly an established poet of considerable prestige and immense popularity. Her readings were attended by hundreds of adoring fans, especially young women, who not only purchased her books but also learned her poems by heart. She was a literary phenomenon, most comparable perhaps to the American Edna St. Vincent Millay, with whom she shared, among other things, an urbane irony and a defiant yet ludic feminism. In addition, these years of more stable employment, during which she taught dramatic declamation to schoolchildren, provided her the opportunity to travel to Europe in 1930 and then again in 1932. She visited the Switzerland of her birth, as well as neighboring Italy and France, yet the most eventful trips were those to Spain where she gave frequent and well-attended readings and conferences. Her travel writings were also published in *La Nación*, Argentina's major newspaper. When in 1933 Federico García Lorca visited Buenos Aires for the opening of his play

Bodas de sangre (Blood Wedding), Storni assisted the performance, together with most of the city's artists and intellectuals, and went on to develop a warm and close friendship with the Andalusian poet (Galán and Gliemmo 318). An affable and gracious man, Lorca demonstrated admiration for Storni, to the point of writing a light-hearted parody of her "combative" poetic style in a letter to his friend Enrique Amorin (ibid.). Furthermore, Storni's affection for Lorca bore artistic fruit in the more experimental, yet equally passionate, homage entitled "Retrato de García Lorca" (Portrait of García Lorca), part of the ground-breaking *Mundo de siete pozos* (World of Seven Wells), and one of the best poems in her entire career.

During these decades of the 1920's and 1930's, other important writers from the Southern Cone who frequented the same literary circles as Storni, essential ones to the formation of *la vanguardia* (the avant-garde) in Latin American letters, included Jorge Luis Borges, Leopoldo Lugones, the previously mentioned Horacio Quiroga, and even Pablo Neruda (in the capacity of Consul to Chile). In fact, the movement called ultraism, one of the principal expressions of *la vanguardia*, was introduced from Europe by Borges himself. Inspired by the French Symbolists and Parnassians, and begun in Spain during the late 1910's, ultraism fostered experimentation in meter, imagery, and symbolism, resulting in intellectual poetry that traditional readers perceived as cold and inscrutable. (This European element in Latin America's *vanguardia* would continue, of course, with the poets of Spain's Generation of '27, with Lorca in particular having an indelible influence on Storni's development.) Nonetheless, these friendships, like those of many writers, were far from congenial and often accompanied by envy and scorn. Borges and other younger writers frequently mocked Storni and belittled her poetry, going so far as to call her washed-up and even questioning her contributions to feminism (Galán and Gliemmo 255). Despite these scathing slights and injuries, Storni found a sense of belonging and kinship among these writers, particularly as males (ibid.), an attitude that becomes poignantly clear in the following quotation: "...I must have lived as a male; I reclaim for myself the morality of a male" (qtd. in Galán and Gliemmo 302).[5]

A weaker person would have crumpled up and withdrawn into solitude, but not Storni who was no sheepish victim, a woman equally adept at scorn and sarcasm, an unconventional woman with an intense and mordant personality. Storni made this strident confession in one of her articles: "Happy people repulse me. Happiness seems to me the most perfect animal state (qtd. in Galán and Gliemmo 175).[6] Most biographers have noted Storni's frequent bouts of depression throughout her adult life, especially severe during her last years of declining health, but she also experienced "strong fits of inspiration" (Galán and Gliemmo 249),[7] a combination that suggests manic depression or bipolar disorder, or what in Storni's time would have been described as mercurial. According to Galán and Gliemmo, Storni "moves surprisingly from crying to laughter, from sadness to joy" (52).[8] Jones points out that "friends were always astonished to see how easily she could swing from a mood of profound depression to one of elation without any apparent transition" (25).

In 1935, after nine years of mostly writing plays for adults and children, plays that were invariably commercial flops, Storni published *Mundo de siete pozos* (World of Seven Wells), the first book of two proclaiming her transformation into a poet of "la nueva generación" (the new generation). Indeed, the influence of *la vanguardia* is radical in both vision and technique, one that constitutes, according to Galán and Gliemmo, "an aesthetic displacement, the search for renewal... one which combines a fondness for known [traditional] forms with poems conceived from an unconventional and rupturing perspective (323).[9] Moreover, Jones argues that "she consciously sought new modes of self-expression to break her former patterns... put[ting] new stress on form rather than content. Like other avant-garde poets, she made a radical departure from traditional styles and adopted, for the first time in her work, the free verse form. Gone was the emotional tone of her former poetry, which she replaced with impersonal, objective themes and abstract ideas" (53). For example, in poems like "El cazador de paisajes" (The Hunter of Landscapes) and "Mañana gris" (Gray Morning), she explored the world more objectively, even dispassionately, discarding the subjectivity of the earlier work which treated nature as a mirror to her moods. No longer did she speak as the Romantic *poetisa* (poetess) but with an androgynous voice of striking resonance. The world she discovered possessed beauty, yet it was also fraught with loneliness, violence, fragmentation, loss; however, one finds moments of whimsy and surrealistic exuberance that recall the work of the English Edith Sitwell, whose many quirky poems make the Waste Land appear less ominous than Eliot's. Storni skillfully used abstract images to evoke complex states of mind. Without rhyme and syllabic meter, the lines flow like jags of water to the cadence of speech or the sense of the image. Perhaps the most successful poems in *Mundo de siete pozos* are those that, according to Galán and Gliemmo, find their strongest and most convincing expression "between the gentle swing of concept and word, the universal and the personal" (325).[10] That same year of 1935 Storni was unfortunately diagnosed with breast cancer and immediately underwent a radical mastectomy. Her summers were spent on the seashore of Mar del Plata in Uruguay, an inspirational setting for many of her nature poems of this period. Nonetheless, the cancer metastasized, and for three years she endured depression, loneliness, and agonizing pain. On the morning of October 25, 1938, she plunged into Mar del Plata, leaving behind a terse suicide note in red ink that said "Me arrojo al mar" (Galán and Gliemmo 368).[11] A few days earlier she had sent out her final poem "Voy a dormir" (I'm Going to Sleep) to La Nación. Those last years of her life she confronted the tragic suicides of Horacio Quiroga and that of his daughter. The writer Leopoldo Lugones, who had been an unswerving critic of her work, also took his life in 1938. Though she was surely haunted by the specter of death, Storni galvanized the discipline and the will to complete her last book of poems Mascarilla y trébol (Mask and Clover), published shortly before her suicide, which many critics judge to be her crowning achievement. These last poems are even more original than those of El mundo de siete pozos, and perhaps their excellence is no surprise at all for a poet who argued that "my best compositions have been produced in times of agony and pain" (qtd. In Delgado 101).[12] This is a poet who had always found death, hers or anyone else's, to be a compelling and congenial Muse, and when read alongside her last poems, those earlier ones like "Presentimiento" ("Premonition") and "Borrada" ("Erased") turn out to be more disquieting and eerie. As Storni wrote in the introductory section called "Breve explicación" (Brief Explanation), the poems of Mascarilla y trébol "gushed from me with a vitality of content and form, almost in a state of trance (the initial impulse of the idea created by itself a loose mode) because I wrote most of them in a few minutes... although polishing them demanded months" (Obras I 394).[13]

These last poems employ experimental techniques like free association that she argued require our "imaginative collaboration" (Obras I 393)[14] if we are to decipher their meaning. Their form is both open and closed, having the fourteen lines of the sonnet but without any rhyme scheme. These "antisonnets," as Storni called them, are taut, intense, and implosive. Syntax is ruptured; metaphors are strange in the manner of the Spanish baroque poet Luis de Góngora y Argote, one of the major influences of Spain's Generation of '27. The often tortured distortions of the world we find in poems like "Ruego a Prometeo" (Plea to Prometheus) and "A Eros" (To Eros) reflect her inner crisis. In the former she imagines herself chained to the god's stone "that grinds night's celestial bodies," and in the latter the deceitful son of Venus "disemboweled... like a doll" and thereafter "tossed... into the mouth of waves." Indeed, these demanding and uncompromising poems are the riskiest of her career, especially for such a ubiquitous poet grown accustomed to public adulation. Jones explains that "her poetry was now generally thought to be hermetic and obscure. She lost a considerable number of her readers"; nevertheless, Storni "was not outwardly concerned... [for] in this last year of her life she seemed to have finally found the courage to shrug at the opinions of her critics..." (48).

No doubt these final years were a period of "deep skepticism... spiritual exhaustion... disillusionment with the world" (Galán and Gliemmo 365).[15] Nonetheless, Jones makes a strong case for this last book's supremacy: "all her disillusionment, her cynicism, her insight, her resolutions to control the passion which she had so often seen as a cruel deception, all her mental efforts to negate her physical and sentimental needs met with failure, until she accepted her impending death and thus saw life in an entirely new perspective" (83). One is persuaded to read *Mascarilla y trébol* as a testament to poetry's ability to heal. We sense that her final poems not only defy death at every turn but are also like rituals exorcising physical and psychological pain.

\

La inquietud del rosal
Restlessness of the Rosebush
(1916)

Yo quiero

Volver a lo que fui, materia acaso
Sin conciencia de ser, como la planta
Gustar la vida y en belleza tanta
Sorber la savia sin quebrar el vaso.

I Want

To go back to what I was, perhaps matter
Without an awareness of being, like a plant.
To savor life, and amidst much beauty
Slurp the sap without breaking the glass.

Fecundidad

¡Mujeres!... La belleza es una forma
Y el óvulo una idea—
¡Triunfe el óvulo!

Dentro de la mentira de la vida
Existe una verdad
Y hay que seguirla.

La verdad es que nada en la Natura
debe perderse.

La tierra que es moral porque procrea
Abre la entraña a la simiente y brota
Dándonos trigo.

El vientre que se da sin reticencias
Pone un soplo de Dios en su pecado.

Son para él las rosas que abre el sol.
Él vibrará como una cuerda loca
Que el Misterio estremece.

El vientre que se niegue será atado
Al carro de la sed eternamente.

¡Mujeres! Sobre el grito de lo bello
Grite el impulso fuerte de la raza.
¡Cada vientre es un cofre!

¿Qué se guarda en las células que tiene?
¿Cuántos óvulos viejos han rodado
Guardándose el misterio que encerraban?

¿Estaba en ellos quien hacía falta?

¡Mujeres! La belleza es una forma
Y el óvulo una idea...

Fruitfulness

Women!... Beauty is a form
And the ovule an idea—
Victory to the ovule!

Within the lie of life
Exists a truth,
And one must follow it.

Truth is that nothing in Nature
Should be lost.

Moral because it procreates,
Earth opens the pith, and the seed sprouts,
Giving us wheat.

The womb that bears without qualms
Puts a puff of God in its sin.

Those sun-split roses are for the womb.
Plucked by Mystery, it will vibrate
Like a mad string.

The womb that refuses will be tied
Eternally to the cart of thirst.

Women! Let the strong impulse
Of our race scream over beauty's shout.
Every womb is a strongbox!

What is kept inside its cells?
How many old ovules have rolled away,
Retaining the mystery they enclosed?

Was the one we needed inside them?

Women! Beauty is a form
And the ovule an idea...

Injusticia

Tenía entonces diez años.
Robaron algún dinero
De las arcas de mi madre.
Fue un domingo... ¡Lo recuerdo!

Se me señaló culpable
Injustamente, y el reto
Que hicieron a mi vergüenza
Se me clavó aquí, ¡muy dentro!

Recuerdo que aquella noche
Tendida sobre mi lecho
Llegó un germen de anarquía
A iniciarse en mi cerebro.

Injustice

I was then ten years old.
They stole some money
From my mother's safe.
On a Sunday... I remember!

I was unjustly declared
Guilty. When they doubted
My honor, scolding words
Pierced me here — very deep!

I remember how that night —
Lying in bed —
A seed of anarchy
Took root in my brain.

Del arrabal

Sofoca el calor; la pieza
Del conventillo malsano
Tiene entornada la puerta…
Ha pasado mediodía,
Es la siesta.

En el cuarto aquel mezquino
Donde todo es de miseria
Dice un poema la cuna
Que mueve al compás la abuela
El niño duerme tranquilo.
Y las rizadas guedejas
Le forman una aureola
Tan bella o quizás más bella
Que la del niño Jesús
Que ampara la cabecera
De la cuna tan humilde
Que sabe decir poemas.
Pasa un órgano en la calle,
Sus acordes tristes suenan
Mezclados con la algazara
De los chicos en la acera.

* * *

El niño sigue durmiendo;
Habla muy quedo la abuela
Y sus palabras son tristes
Porque son muchas sus penas:
"¡Niño Jesús, tú que guardas
Del nene la cabecera,
No dejes que el nene sufra!"

* * *

Sofoca el calor; la pieza
Del conventillo malsano
Tiene entornada la puerta…

From the Poor Outskirts

The heat suffocates.
The filthy bedroom
Has its door ajar...
It is past noon,
Time for the siesta.

In that paltry room
Reeking of poverty,
The cradle recites a poem
As the grandmother rocks
The child to placid sleep.
And the curled locks form
An aureole as beautiful—
Perhaps more beautiful—
Than that of Baby Jesus
Who protects the head
Of such a humble crib
That knows how to recite poems.
An organ goes by the street,
Its sad chords mixed
With the joyous shouts
Of kids on the sidewalk.

* * *

The boy keeps on sleeping.
The grandmother speaks
Very softly, her words sad,
Her sorrows many:
"Baby Jesus, who guards
The little boy by his cradle,
Do not let him suffer!"

* * *

The heat suffocates.
The filthy bedroom
Has its door ajar...

El dulce daño
The Sweet Hurt
(1918)

Lluvia pasada

Siete días largos la lluvia monótona
Golpeó mi ventana.
Siete días largos.
El corazón mismo se llenó de agua.

Nubes en los labios,
En el pecho sombras,
Libros en las manos, las mejillas blancas.
Siete días largos...
Las aceras húmedas, los negros paraguas.

Hoy nacieron cuatro rosas purpurinas
Y están en mi cara.
Oro de los cielos puso ruiseñores
En todas las jaulas.

Sangre borbotea, los pies no se apoyan,
La carne es estrecha y el alma rebalsa;
Fluido que ahoga me rodea el cuerpo:
Abiertos los poros no retengo el alma.

¡Oh lástima, lástima!
Tanta primavera que no logra taza
    Para ser bebida.
Tanta primavera que no logra llama
    Para ser quemada.

Tú, ¿dónde te ocultas, tú, que no has logrado
Todavía telas, redes, cribas, mallas,
Donde enredarían mis flores-azules
Vencidas de amores a dulces palabras?

¿Dónde las dos manos de acero y de seda
Que me tomarían en esta mañana
Solar, para nunca soltarme; las manos
Que habrían de hacerme roja siendo blanca?

¡Oh, mi primavera que logró su llama.
¡Oh, mi primavera en sus manos fuertes
Perdida y gustada!

Past Rain

For seven long days the monotonous rain
Beat on my window.
Seven long days.
My heart flooded with water.

Clouds on my lips,
Shadows in my breast,
Books in my hands, my cheeks white.
Seven long days...
Wet sidewalks, black umbrellas.

Today four purple roses were born,
And they are in my face.
The sky's gold placed nightingales
In all cages.

Blood bubbles, feet wobble.
The flesh is narrow, the soul overflows.
The drowning fluid surrounds my body.
Pores open. I cannot hold back the soul.

Oh, pity, pity!
So much spring that does not gain the cup
    For drinking.
So much spring that does not gain the flame
    For burning.

Where do you hide, you who have not yet
Gained the cloths, nets, sieves, meshes
That would entangle my blue flowers,
Defeated in love by sweet words?

Where are the two hands of steel and silk
That would grab me this sunlit
Morning and never let go, hands
That would turn me red being white?

Oh, my spring that gains its flame.
Oh, my spring in its strong hands,
Lost and tasted!

Dos palabras

Esta noche al oído me has dicho dos palabras
Comunes. Dos palabras cansadas
De ser dichas. Palabras
Que de viejas son nuevas.

Dos palabras tan dulces, que la luna que andaba
Filtrando entre las ramas
Se detuvo en mi boca. Tan dulces dos palabras
Que una hormiga pasea por mi cuello y no intento
Moverme para echarla.

Tan dulces dos palabras
Que digo sin quererlo—¡oh!, qué bella, la vida!—
Tan dulces y tan mansas
Que aceites olorosos sobre el cuerpo derraman.

Tan dulces y tan bellas
Que nerviosos, mis dedos,
Se mueven hacia el cielo imitando tijeras.

Oh, mis dedos quisieran
Cortar estrellas.

Two Words

Tonight you've whispered in my ear
Two common words. Two tired words.
Words so old they are new.

Two words so sweet that moonlight
Seeping through the branches
Touched my mouth. Two words so sweet
I dare not move to swat
An ant strolling on my neck.

Two words so sweet
I say it without meaning to: Oh, how beautiful life is.
So sweet and so tame
They pour fragrant oils on my body.

So sweet and so beautiful
My nervous fingers
Move toward heaven imitating scissors.

Oh, my fingers would like
To cut stars.

El llamado

Es noche, tal silencio
Que si Dios parpadeara
Lo oyera. Yo paseo.
En la selva, mis plantas
Pisan la hierba fresca

Que salpica rocío.
Las estrellas me hablan,
Y me beso los dedos,
Finos de luna blanca.

De pronto soy herida...
Y el corazón se para,
Se enroscan mis cabellos
Mis espaldas se agrandan;
Oh, mis dedos florecen,
Mis miembros echan alas,
Voy a morir ahogada
Por luces y fragancias...

Es que en medio a la selva
Tu voz dulce me llama...

The Call

Nighttime, so quiet
That if God were to blink
I'd hear him. I stroll.
In the jungle, my plants
Tread the fresh grass

That spatters dew.
Stars speak to me,
And I kiss my fingers,
Delicate as white moons.

Suddenly I'm wounded...
My heart stops, hairs coil,
My back grows larger;
Oh, my fingers flower,
My limbs sprout wings,
And I'll die drowned
By lights and fragrances...

Because amidst the jungle
Your sweet voice calls to me...

Ladrona

Me llegaré al jardín donde reposas,
Me bañaré en tu estanque
Y robaré tus rosas.

Mi cuerpo echará lirios cuando arranque,
En tanto que reposas,
Todas tus rosas.

Cuando, ladrona, trepe por los hierros
Huyendo del jardín suelta tus perros.

En mis brazos tus rosas,
Desgárrenme las carnes temblorosas
Tus blancos perros
Cabe tus hierros.

Thief

I will reach the garden where you repose,
Bathe in your pond,
Steal your roses.

My body will sprout lilies
When I pull all your roses
While you repose.

When I, the thief, flee your garden,
Climbing the iron fence, release your dogs.

Let your white dogs tear
My quivering flesh.
In my arms your roses will fit
Through the iron railings.

Transfusión

La vida tuya sangre mía abona
Y te amo a muerte, te amo; si pudiera
Bajo los cielos negros te comiera
El corazón con dientes de leona.

Antes de conocerte era ladrona
Y ahora soy menguada prisionera.
¡Cómo luces de bien, mi primavera!
¡Cómo brilla en tu frente mi corona!

Sangre que es mía en tus pupilas arde
Y entre tus labios pone cada tarde
Las uvas dulces con que Pan convida.

Y en tanto, flor sin aire, flor en gruta,
Me exprimo toda en ti como una fruta
Y entre tus manos se me va la vida.

Transfusion

Your life fertilizes my blood.
I love you, love you to death, and if I could
I would eat your heart with teeth
Of a lioness beneath dark skies.

Before I met you I was a thief
And now I am a wretched prisoner.
How well you look, my spring!
How my crown burns on your forehead!

Blood that is mine burns in your pupils,
And each afternoon it places between
Your lips those sweet grapes, Pan's offering.

Meanwhile, I—airless flower, cave flower—
Squeeze myself into you like a fruit,
My life fading between your hands.

Tú me quieres blanca

Tú me quieres alba,
Me quieres de espumas,
Me quieres de nácar.
Que sea azucena,
Sobre todas, casta.
De perfume tenue.
Corola cerrada.

Ni un rayo de luna
Filtrado me haya.
Ni una margarita
Se diga mi hermana.
Tú me quieres nívea,
Tú me quieres blanca,
Tú me quieres alba.

Tú que hubiste todas
Las copas a mano,
De frutos y mieles
Los labios morados.
Tú que en el banquete
Cubierto de pámpanos
Dejaste las carnes
Festejando a Baco.
Tú que en los jardines
Negros del Engaño
Vestido de rojo
Corriste al Estrago.
Tú que el esqueleto
Conservas intacto
No sé todavía
Por cuáles milagros,
Me pretendes blanca
(Dios te lo perdone)
Me pretendes casta
(Dios te lo perdone)
¡Me pretendes alba!

Huye hacia los bosques;
Vete a la montaña;
Límpiate la boca;
Vive en las cabañas;
Toca con las manos
La tierra mojada;
Alimenta el cuerpo
Con raíz amarga;
Bebe de las rocas;
Duerme sobre escarcha;
Renueva tejidos
Con salitre y agua;
Habla con los pájaros
Y lévate al alba.
Y cuando las carnes
Te sean tornadas,
Y cuando hayas puesto
En ellas el alma
Que por las alcobas
Se quedó enredada,
Entonces, buen hombre,
Preténdeme blanca,
Preténdeme nívea,
Preténdeme casta.

You Wish I Were Fair

You wish I were dawn,
You wish I were seafoam,
You wish I were nacre.
To be a lily.
Above all others, chaste.
Of faint perfume.
Closed corolla.

Not even a sieved
Moon ray finds me.
Not even a daisy
Can be called my sister.
You wish I were snow,
You wish I were fair,
You wish I were dawn.

You who had all cups
Within easy reach,
Your lips purple
From fruits and honey.
You who wasted away
Banqueting Bacchus
At the feast table
Covered with tendrils.
You who raced to Ruin
In the black garden
Of red-clothed Deceit.
You who preserves
The skeleton whole,
Though I do not yet know
By what miracles
You pretend I am fair
(May God forgive you)
You pretend I am chaste
(May God forgive you)
You pretend I am dawn!

Flee to the forests;
Go to the mountain;
Wipe your mouth;
Live in wood shacks;
Touch the wet earth
With your hands;
Feed your body
With bitter roots;
Drink from the rocks;
Sleep over frost;
Revive tissues
With saltpeter and water.
Talk to birds,
Rise at dawn.
And when your flesh
Has been returned to you,
And you have placed
Inside it your soul
That got entangled
In bedrooms,
Then—good man—
Pretend I am fair,
Pretend I am snow,
Pretend I am chaste.

Presentimiento

Tengo el presentimiento que he de vivir muy poco.
Esta cabeza mía se parece al crisol,
Purifica y consume,
Pero sin una queja, sin asomo horror,
Para acabarme quiero que una tarde sin nubes,
Bajo el límpido sol,
Nazca de un gran jazmín una víbora blanca
Que dulce, dulcemente, me pique el corazón.

Premonition

I have the feeling that I won't live long.
This head of mine resembles a crucible
That purifies and consumes
With no complaint or trace of horror.
I dream the white viper
Of my destruction. One cloudless
Afternoon, the sun limpid,
She will be born from a grand jasmine
And sweetly, so sweetly, bite my heart.

Cuadros y ángulos

Casas enfiladas, casas enfiladas,
Casas enfiladas.
Cuadrados, cuadrados, cuadrados.
Casas enfiladas.
Las gentes ya tienen el alma cuadrada,
Ideas en fila
Y ángulo en la espalda.
Yo misma he vertido ayer una lágrima,
Dios mío, cuadrada.

Squares and Angles

Houses in rows, houses in rows,
Houses in rows.
Squares, squares, squares,
Houses in rows.
People's souls are already squared,
Ideas in single file,
And our backs angled.
Yesterday I shed a tear—
Oh my God—squared.

Parásitos

Jamás pensé que Dios tuviera alguna forma.
Absoluta su vida; y absoluta su norma.
Ojos no tuvo nunca: mira con las estrellas.
Manos no tuvo nunca: golpea con los mares.
Lengua no tuvo nunca: habla con las centellas.
Te diré, no te asombres;
Sé que tiene parásitos: las cosas y los hombres.

Parasites

I never thought God had any form.
Absolute his life, absolute his rule.
He never had eyes, watches with stars.
He never had hands, punches with seas.
He never had a tongue, talks with thunderbolts.
I will tell you, do not startle;
I know He has parasites: things and men.

Irremediablemente
Irremediably
(1919)

Ven...

Ven esta noche amado; tengo el mundo
Sobre mi corazón... La vida estalla...
Ven esta noche amado; tengo miedo
De mi alma.

¡Oh no puedo llorar! Dame tus manos
Y verás cómo el alma se resbala
Tranquilamente; cómo el alma cae
En una lágrima.

Come…

Come tonight, love. I have the world
On top of my heart… Life explodes…
Come tonight, love; I am afraid
Of my soul.

Oh, I cannot cry! Give me your hands
And you will see how the soul
Slips calmly; how the soul falls
In a teardrop.

Peso ancestral

Tú me dijiste: no lloró mi padre;
Tú me dijiste: no lloró mi abuelo;
No han llorado los hombres de mi raza,
Eran de acero.

Así diciendo te brotó una lágrima
Y me cayó en la boca... más veneno:
Yo no he bebido nunca en otro vaso
Así pequeño.

Débil mujer, pobre mujer que entiende,
Dolor de siglos conocí al beberlo:
Oh, el alma mía soportar no puede
Todo su peso.

Ancestral Weight

You told me my father did not weep;
Told me my grandfather did not weep;
The men of my race have not wept.
They were of iron.

As you spoke a tear welled up
And fell on my mouth... more poison:
I have never drunk from another
Glass this small.

Weak woman, poor understanding woman,
I knew the pain of centuries when I drank
From it. Oh, my soul cannot support
All its weight.

Hombre pequeñito

Hombre pequeñito, hombre pequeñito,
Suelta a tu canario que quiere volar...
Yo soy el canario, hombre pequeñito,
Déjame saltar.

Estuve en tu jaula, hombre pequeñito,
Hombre pequeñito que jaula me das.
Digo pequeñito porque no me entiendes,
Ni me entenderás.

Tampoco te entiendo, pero mientras tanto
Ábreme la jaula que quiero escapar;
Hombre pequeñito, te amé media hora,
No me pidas más.

Little Man

Little man, little man, let go
Your canary who wants to fly...
I'm that canary, little man,
Let me leap.

I was in your cage, little man.
Little man, what cage you give me.
I say little since you don't understand me,
Nor will you.

I don't understand you either, but meanwhile
Open the cage: I want to escape;
Little man, I loved you half an hour.
Don't ask for more.

Sepulcro polvoriento

Cuando me falta la palabra tuya
Suelo ser un sepulcro polvoriento
Alzado sobre piedras descarnadas:
Mundos arriba y en la piedra el viento.

Oh, me estrujaran toda y ni una gota
Soltara el cuerpo como el alma seco;
Sepulcro sobre piedras, si me faltas,
Sepulcro milenario y polvoriento.

Dusty Tomb

When I miss your words
I become a dusty tomb
Lifted by gaunt stones.
Worlds above; the wind in stone.

Oh, they will wrinkle me, and my body,
Dry as the soul, will not shed a drop.
A tomb on stones, if you are gone,
Dusty and a thousand years old.

Languidez
Languor
(1920)

Domingos

En los domingos, cuando están las calles
Del centro quietas,
Alguna vez camino, y las oscuras,
Cerradas puertas
De los negocios, son como sepulcros
Sobre veredas.

Si yo golpeara en un domingo d'ésos
Las frías puertas,
De agrisado metal, sonido hueco
Me respondiera...
Se prolongara luego por las calles
Grises y rectas.

¿Qué hacen en los estantes, acostadas,
Las negras piezas
De géneros? Estantes, como nichos,
Guardan las muertas
Cosas, de los negocios adormidos
Bajo sus puertas.

Una que otra persona por las calles
Solas, se encuentra:
Un hombre, una mujer, manchan el aire
Con su presencia,
Y sus pasos se sienten uno a uno
En la vereda.

Detrás de las paredes las personas
¿Mueren o sueñan?
Camino por las calles: se levantan
Mudas barreras
A mis costados: dos paredes largas
Y paralelas.

Vueltas y vueltas doy por esas calles;
Por donde quiera,
Me siguen las paredes silenciosas,
Y detrás d'ellas
En vano saber quiero si los hombres
Mueren o sueñan.

Sundays

Sundays, when downtown streets
Are quiet,
I sometimes stroll, and the dark,
Closed doors
Of shops are tombs
On the sidewalk.

One of those Sundays if I knocked
On the cold doors
Of grayish metal, a hollow sound
Would answer back...
And it would later spread through
The gay and straight streets.

What are the bolts of black cloth doing
Lying on the shelves?
Like tombs in a wall, the shelves keep
The dead things
Of stores asleep beneath
Their doors.

On the streets one finds one person
Alone, or another:
A man and a woman stain the air
With their presence,
And their steps are felt one by one
On the sidewalk.

Do people die or dream
Behind walls?
I walk the streets and mute barriers
Rise up along
My sides: two long and parallel
Walls.

I go around and around those streets.
Everywhere
The silent walls follow me,
And behind them
I wish to know, in vain, if men
Die or dream.

Siesta

Sobre la tierra seca
El sol quemando cae:
Zumban los moscardones
Y las grietas se abren…
El viento no se mueve.
Desde la tierra sale
Un vaho como de horno:
Se abochorna la tarde
Y resopla cocida
Bajo el plomo del aire…
Ahogo, pesadez,
Cielo blanco; ni un ave.

Se oye un pequeño ruido:
Entre las pajas mueve
Su cuerpo amosaicado
Una larga serpiente.
Ondula con dulzura.

Por las piedras calientes
Se desliza, pesada,
Después de su banquete
De dulces y pequeños
Pájaros aflautados
Que le abultan el vientre.

Se enrosca poco a poco,
Muy pesada y muy blanda
Poco a poco se duerme
Bajo la tarde blanca.
¿Hasta cuándo su sueño?
Ya no se escucha nada.

Larga siesta de víbora
Duerme también mi alma.

Siesta

The scorching sun
Sets on the dry land:
Botflies buzz
And the fissures open...
The wind doesn't move.
An ovenlike haze
Rises from the earth;
Abashed, the afternoon
Puffs, boiled beneath
The lead of air...
Breathless, heavy,
White sky, no birds.

A slight noise is heard.
A large snake—
Its body a mosaic—
Slithers through straw,
Undulating sweetly.

It slides against
The hot stones,
Heavy from a banquet
Of sweets and small
Flute-voiced birds
That swell its belly.

It coils, bit by bit,
Very heavy, very soft,
Then slowly falls asleep
In the white afternoon.
Until when will it dream?
Nothing is heard.

My soul also sleeps
The snake's long siesta.

Rosales de suburbio

Claro, como llegó la primavera,
Sobre las pobres casas
De latas y maderas,
De los suburbios, buen rosal que trepas,
Te has cubierto de rosas.

Si tú fueras
Como los hombres, oh rosal, sin duda,
Como ellos, prefirieras
Para bien florecer las ricas casas,
Las paredes lujosas; y desiertas
Dejaras las paredes de los pobres.

Pero no eres así.
La dulce tierra
Te basta en cualquier parte y te es lo mismo,
Para tu suerte. Acaso, tú prefieras
Las modestas casuchas donde luces
Mejor, enredadera.
Único adorno que no cuesta nada...
(El agua, buenas rosas, todavía
Se baja de los cielos sin gabelas.)

En las bellas mañanas, cuando miras
Las ventanas abiertas,

Tus brazos verdes y jugosos, buscan
El espacio sin vidrios y penetran
Al interior del cuarto: —¡Buenos días!
Tus corolas intentan
Decir con sus rosados labiezuelos
A la modesta pieza.

Slum Rosebushes

Of course, since spring has arrived
On the poor houses
Of tin and scrap wood in the outskirts,
You, beautiful climbing bush,
Have covered yourself in roses.

If you were
Like men, O rosebush, you'd no doubt
Prefer for good blooming
Rich houses, their walls luxurious,
And you'd then leave barren
The walls of the poor.

But you're not like this.
The sweet earth
Is enough for you anywhere, and it suits you
The same for luck. Maybe you'd prefer
Those modest hovels where you look
Better as a creeper.
The only decoration that costs nothing…
(Good roses, water still falls
From the sky without taxes.)

Beautiful mornings, when you gaze
At open windows,

Your green and juicy arms
Search the glassless space and penetrate
The inside of the room: Good morning,
Your corollas try to say
To the modest bedroom
With their rosy lips.

Luego, si muy risueño
Se te acerca
El niño sucio de azulados ojos
Y carnes prietas,
Te haces el que no entiendes y no miras;
Pero entiendes y miras, y le sueltas
Con mucho disimulo,
Como quien no quisiera,
Sobre sus rizos de oro, una corola
Sabiamente deshecha.

El niño, entonces, de suburbio, luce
En la rubia cabeza
La corona divina. No la siente
Porque nada le pesa
Y como un Eros, haraposo, canta,
Y corriendo se aleja.

Later, if the dirty boy
Of bluish eyes
And dark flesh gets too
Cheerfully close,
You feign ignorance and do not look;
Yet you do understand and look.
As if you could not help it,
You stealthily place on top
of his golden curls
A corolla wisely pulled apart.

Then the slum boy shows off
The divine crown
In his blond head. He does not feel it,
For nothing feels heavy.
Like some ragged Eros he sings
And runs away.

Tristeza

Al lado de la gran ciudad se tiende
El río. Cieno
Muy líquido. Parece
Que no se mueve, que está muerto, pero
Se mueve.

Justamente como es cieno
Se va buscando el mar azul y limpio,
Y hacia él, muy pesado, mueve el cuerpo,
Sin detenerse nunca; siempre otro
Aunque parezca el mismo.

Río muerto,
Desde esta torre, mientras muere el día,
Ensoñando lo veo
Que se ensancha en un vasto semicírculo
Y se pierde allá lejos
Bajo la bruma gris, cortada a ratos
Por un triángulo blanco.

Sobre el puerto
Buques y buques se amontonan, y éstos
Parecen peces monstruos afanados
Sobre un mismo alimento.

Sadness

Beside the great city
The river sprawls,
Soft silted. It seems
Motionless, dead, yet
It moves.

Precisely because it is silty,
The river seeks out the sea, blue and limpid,
A heavy body that moves
Without stopping, always another,
Though it seems the same.

Day wanes, and I dream
From this tower, watching the dead
River swell to a vast half-circle,
Disappearing far into the gray
Sea mist that is sometimes sliced
By a white triangle.

Ships and ships pile up
On the port, as if monstrous fish
Had set upon the same prey.

Borrada

El día que me muera, la noticia
Ha de seguir las prácticas usadas,
Y de oficina en oficina al punto.
Por los registros seré yo buscada.

Y allá muy lejos, en un pueblecito
Que está durmiendo al sol en la montaña,
Sobre mi nombre, en un registro viejo,
Mano que ignoro trazará una raya.

Erased

The day I die, the news should
Follow the usual practice:
To the end from office to office.
I will be searched for in records.

And far away, in a little town
That sun-dozes on the mountain,
A hand I do not know will draw
A line across my name in an old record.

Sed

Mucho tiempo hace ya que el sol calcina
La tierra y está blanca y muy reseca;
No puede más: aguanta, aguanta, pero
Atormentada por las largas siestas
Un grito desde adentro se le sube
Y se parte, violenta, en una grieta.

La muerta boca de los labios secos
Que ha brotado en la tierra
Se estira al cielo y ¡agua!
Ya pronunciar intenta.

Thirst

It's been a long time since the sun
Has scorched the earth, now so white, arid;
She's had enough, putting up, putting up,
But long naps torment her,
A scream rises from deep below,
And she tears into a chasm.

The dry lips' dead mouth
That burst from the earth
Stretches to the sky
And tries to utter Water!

La pesca

Al borde de la vida,
Los hombres, en pescar,
Se pasan todo el tiempo:
Quién menos y quién más.

Atropellando vienen
Sus puestos a ocupar,
Traen grandes carnadas
Y piensan: picarán.

Arriba el cielo limpio
Muy quietecito está
Y abajo, con su anzuelo,
Todos vienen y van.

Pescador: no te apures,
Deja el anzuelo en paz,
La muerte, ten seguro,
No se te escapará.

Fishing

Some less, some more,
Men spend all their time
On the fringe of life
When they go fishing.

They trample over everyone
To take over the spots.
Bring huge baits
And think: they will bite.

The sky above
Is clear and still;
Fish below come
And go with the bait.

Do not hurry, fisherman,
Leave the bait in peace.
Be assured that death
Will not spare you.

Siglo XX

Me estoy consumiendo en vida,
Gastando sin hacer nada,
Entre las cuatro paredes
Simétricas de mi casa.

¡Eh, obreros! ¡Traed las picas!
Paredes y techos caigan,
Me mueva el aire la sangre,
Me queme el sol las espaldas.

Mujer soy del siglo XX;
Paso el día recostada
Mirando, desde mi cuarto,
Cómo se mueve una rama.

Se está quemando la Europa
Y estoy mirando sus llamas
Con la misma indiferencia
Con que contemplo esa rama.

Tú, el que pasas: no me mires
De arriba abajo; mi alma
Grita su crimen, la tuya
Lo esconde bajo palabras.

The 20th Century

I am wasting away in life
Within the four symmetrical
Walls of my house,
Consumed but doing nothing.

Hey, workers! Bring the picks!
Come down walls and roofs.
Let the air stir my blood.
Let the sun burn my back.

I am woman of the 20th century,
Spend all day in my room
Lying down and watching
How a branch moves.

Europe is burning down
And I'm looking at its flames
With the same indifference
That I contemplate that branch.

You, passerby, don't stare
At me up and down;
My soul screams its crime.
Yours hides it beneath words.

Ocre
Ocher
(1925)

Palabras a Rubén Darío

Bajo sus lomos rojos, en la oscura caoba,
Tus libros duermen. Sigo los últimos autores:
Otras formas me atraen, otros nuevos colores
Y a tus Fiestas paganas la corriente me roba.

Goza de estilos fieros—anchos dientes de loba.
De otros sobrios, prolijos—cipreses veladores.
De otros blancos y finos—columnas bajo flores.
De otros ácidos y ocres—tempestades de alcoba.

Ya te había olvidado y al azar te retomo,
Y a los primeros versos se levanta del tomo
Tu fresco y fino aliento de mieles olorosas.

Amante al que se vuelve como la vez primera:
Eres la boca que allá, en la primavera,
Nos licuara en las venas todo un bosque de rosas.

Words for Rubén Darío

On their red spines, in the dark mahogany,
Your books sleep. I follow the latest authors:
Other forms attract me, newer colors, yet the current
Steals me toward your pagan festivals.

Your verse enjoys fierce styles: wide she-wolf's teeth.
Those that are sober and prolix: cypress night lamps.
Those that are white and fine: flowery columns.
Those that are acid and ocher: bedroom tempests.

I had already forgotten you, yet by chance take
You up again, and as I read the book's first verses,
Your breath rises up, fragrant as honey.

Like the lost lover returning that first time,
You are the mouth that in the spring
Will liquify a forest of roses in our veins.

Versos a la tristeza de Buenos Aires

Tristes calles derechas, agrisadas e iguales,
Por donde asoma, a veces, un pedazo de cielo,
Sus fachadas oscuras y el asfalto del suelo
Me apagaron los tibios sueños primaverales.

Cuánto vagué por ellas, distraída, empapada
En el vaho grisáceo, lento, que las decora.
De su monotonía mi alma padece ahora.
—¡Alfonsina! —No llames. Ya no respondo a nada.

Si en una de tus casas, Buenos Aires, me muero
Viendo en días de otoño tu cielo prisionero
No me será sorpresa la lápida pesada.

Que entre tus calles rectas, untadas de su río
Apagado, brumoso, desolante y sombrío,
Cuando vagué por ellas, ya estaba yo enterrada.

Lines to the Sadness of Buenos Aires

Sad streets—straight, gray, identical—
Where sometimes a chunk of sky peeks,
Whose asphalt and sooty facades
Snuffed my lukewarm dreams of spring.

How often I idled in them, distracted, soaked
In the gray, sluggish haze that adorns them. My soul
Now suffers from their monotony. *Alfonsina!*
Don't call back. (I don't respond to anything anymore.)

Buenos Aires, if I die in one of your houses,
Watching your imprisoned sky in autumn days,
I wouldn't be surprised by the heavy headstone.

For I was already buried when I idled
In your straight streets, smeared by their river:
Snuffed, fogged, desolate, and somber.

Inútil soy

Por seguir de las cosas el compás,
A veces quise, en este siglo activo,
Pensar, luchar, vivir con lo que vivo,
Ser en el mundo algún tornillo más.

Pero, atada al ensueño seductor,
De mi instinto volví al oscuro pozo,
Pues, como algún insecto perezoso
Y voraz, yo nací para el amor.

Inútil soy, pesada, torpe, lenta.
Mi cuerpo, al sol, tendido, se alimenta
Y sólo vivo bien en el verano,
Cuando la selva huele y la enroscada
Serpiente duerme en tierra calcinada;
Y la fruta se baja hasta mi mano.

I Am Useless

Because of keeping to the tempo
Of this bustling century, I wanted
At times to think, struggle, bear each day,
And be just another screw in the world.

But tied to seductive daydreaming,
And because of my nature, I returned
To the dark well, for I was born to love
Like some lazy and voracious insect.

I am useless, annoying, clumsy, slow.
My body feeds as it lies in the sun,
And I only live well in summer
When the woods smell, the coiled
Snake slumbers in scorched earth,
And fruit drops down to my hand.

Femenina

Baudelaire: yo me acuerdo de tus Flores del mal
En que hablas de una horrible y perversa judía
Acaso como el cuerpo de las serpientes fría,
En lágrimas indocta, y en el daño genial.

Pero a su lado no eras tan pobre, Baudelaire:
De sus formas vendidas, y de su cabellera
Y de sus ondulantes caricias de pantera,
Hombre al cabo, lograbas un poco de placer.

Pero yo, femenina, Baudelaire, ¿qué me hago
De este hombre calmo y prieto como un gélido lago,
Oscuro de ambiciones y ebrio de vanidad,

En cuyo enjuto pecho salino no han podido
Ni mi cálido aliento, ni mi beso rendido,
Hacer brotar un poco de generosidad?

Female

Baudelaire, I remember your *Flowers of Evil*
In which you talk about a horrible, perverse Jewess,
As if perhaps her body were cold like a snake's,
Her weeping crude, her hurtfulness brilliant.

Beside her you were not so poor, Baudelaire.
Being a man, you still gained some pleasure
From the sold parts of her figure, her mane,
Her undulating caresses of panther.

But as a female, Baudelaire, what should I do
With this man, stolid and stiff as an icy lake,
Dark in ambition, and drunk with vanity,

In whose gaunt, salty chest my warm breath
And my devoted kisses have failed
To sprout even just a bit of generosity?

Palabras a Delmira Agustini

Estás muerta y tu cuerpo, bajo uruguayo manto,
Descansa de su fuego, se limpia de su llama.
Sólo desde tus libros tu roja lengua llama
Como cuando vivías, al amor y al encanto.

Hoy, si un alma de tantas, sentenciosa y oscura,
Con palabras pesadas va a sangrarte el oído,
Encogida en tu pobre cajoncito roído
No puedes contestarle desde tu sepultura.

Pero sobre tu pecho, para siempre deshecho,
Comprensivo vigila, todavía, mi pecho,
Y si ofendida lloras por tus cuencas abiertas,

Tus lágrimas heladas, con mano tan liviana
Que más que mano amiga parece mano hermana,
Te enjugo dulcemente las tristes cuencas muertas.

Words for Delmira Agustini

In death your body, under a Uruguayan shawl,
Rests from its fire, cleanses away its flame.
Only from your books does your red tongue call out,
As when you lived—to love, to enchantment.

Today, if one of those dark, self-righteous souls
Were to bleed your ear with irksome words,
You would be unable to respond from your grave,
Coiled inside your poor, gnawed-out little box.

Yet my breast still keeps vigil over yours,
Forever torn apart. And if offended,
You would weep frozen tears from gaping eyes.

I would sweetly wipe those sad and dead
Eye sockets, my hand so light
It would seem more a sister's than a friend's.

Dejad dormir a Cristo

Dejad dormir a Cristo: desde el duro madero
Ha veinte siglos oye: "Interceded por nos".
De su pecho de palo, sensible al lacrimero,
Ya extrajisteis, sobrado, lo que cabe en un dios.

Dejad dormir a Cristo y si estáis en naufragio
Hacia otro calmo puerto desamarrad las velas
Que, obligado a dentista por el mayor sufragio,
Bastante os ha curado los dolores de muelas.

Veneno le pedisteis para mojar la flecha,
Propicia sombra y viento para encender la mecha,
Lo bajasteis al lecho que el diablo presidía.

¿Quién dijo que era un pozo jamás desagotado?
Huyendo de los hombres, por sobre algún tejado,
Habréis de verlo, en fuga, dejar la cruz vacía.

Let Christ Go to Sleep

Let Christ go to sleep. From the hard timbers,
He's heard for twenty centuries: "Intercede for us."
From his wooden breast, sensitive to tears,
You've already sucked more than what a god can hold.

Let Christ go to sleep, and if you're about to wreck,
Turn your sails toward another calmer port.
He's cured your aching teeth quite enough too,
Forced to become a dentist by your pleading.

You begged him for poison to tip the arrow,
Favorable winds and shade to light the fuse,
And you brought him down to the devil's bed.

Who said he was a well that never dries up?
You've seen him on some rooftop fleeing
From mankind, the empty cross left behind.

Una

Es alta y es perfecta, de radiadas pupilas
Azules, donde acecha, perezosa, una Eva.
Su piel es piel de fruta. Su blanca carne nieva
Y sus trenzas se tuercen como gruesas anguilas.

Un bosque de oro crece en sus blancas axilas.
De los árboles rompe la yema fina y nueva.
Su boca es de la muerte la tenebrosa cueva.
Su risa daña el pecho de las aves tranquilas.

Pasó ayer a mi lado, las caderas redondas,
Los duros muslos tensos soliviando las blondas,
Los labios purpurados, y miedo tuve al verla,

Pues, de tal modo es ella, ya la predestinada
Que, se comprende al verla, camina, abandonada,
Hacia el hombre primero que debe poseerla.

The First One

Tall and perfect, radiant blue pupils,
A lazy Eve lies in wait. She has the skin
Of a fruit. Her white flesh sheds
Snow. Her braids twist like thick eels.

A forest of gold grows in her white armpits.
She tears the fresh, white bud from trees.
Her mouth is death's gloomy cave.
Her laughter hurts the breasts of calm birds.

She passed by me yesterday, her hips round,
The thighs hard and tense, their blonde hairs
Standing on end, the lips purplish. I feared her,

For she's already the predestined one,
Whom we realize walks—abandoned—
Toward the first man who will possess her.

La palabra

Naturaleza: gracias por este don supremo
Del verso, que me diste;
Yo soy la mujer triste
A quien Caronte ya mostró su remo.

¿Qué fuera de mi vida sin la dulce palabra?
Como el óxido labra
Sus arabescos ocres,
Yo me grabé en los hombres, sublimes o mediocres.

Mientras vaciaba el pomo, caliente, de mi pecho,
No sentía el acecho,
Torvo y feroz, de la sirena negra.

Me salí de mi carne, gocé el goce más alto:
Oponer una frase de basalto
Al genio oscuro que nos desintegra.

The Word

Nature, thank you for this supreme gift
Of poetry you gave me;
I am the sad woman
To whom Charon already showed his oar.

Where would my life be without the sweet word?
Just as rust etches
Its ocher arabesques,
I engraved myself onto men, sublime or mediocre.

And as I emptied the warm jar of my breast,
I did not sense the lurking
Black siren: ferocious, foreboding.

I came out of my skin, reveled in the highest
Pleasure: to oppose the basalt
Rhetoric of the dark genius who disintegrates us.

Mundo de siete pozos
World of Seven Wells
(1935)

Ojo

Reposa.
El crepúsculo
muere más
allí, donde, pájaro quieto,
aguarda.

Mares tristes,
apretados,
mueven
en él
sus olas.

Los paisajes
del día
lo navegan
lentos.

Tímidas,
las primeras estrellas
lloran
su luz insabora
en la pupila fija

En el fondo oscuro
largas hileras humanas
se le desplazan
incesantemente:

Parten
en distintas
direcciones;
retroceden;
retroceden:
tocan
los primeros
hombres:

Gimen porque nace el sol.
Gimen porque muere el sol...

Todo está allí,
apretado en la cuenca,
donde,
pájaro quieto,
aguarda.

Eye

The eye rests.
Twilight dies
where a still
bird awaits.

Sad seas
—cramped—
toss their
waves
inside
the eye.

The day's
landscapes
slowly
navigate it.

Inside the fixed pupil,
those timid
first stars
mewl
vapid light.

In the dark depths
long rows of humans
jostle the eye
incessantly.

They split up
in different
directions,
falling back,
falling back,
touching
the first
humans:

They moan because the sun is born.
Moan because the sun dies...

Everything is there,
cramped in
the eye socket,
where a still
bird awaits.

Palabras degolladas

Palabras degolladas,
caídas de mis labios
sin nacer;
estranguladas vírgenes
sin sol posible;
pesadas de deseos,
henchidas...

Deformadoras de mi boca
en el impulso de asomar
y el pozo del vacío
al caer...
Desnatadoras de mi miel celeste,
apretada en vosotras
en coronas floridas.

Desangrada en vosotras
—no nacidas—
redes del más aquí y el mas allá,
medialunas,
peces descarnados,
pájaros sin alas,
serpientes desvertebradas...
No perdones,
corazón.

Throat-Slashed Words

You fall from my lips,
throats slashed
before birth,
choked virgins
who will never
see the sun,
loaded with wants,
swollen...

Driven to gaze the light,
you deform my mouth,
and when you fall
into the well
of emptiness...
you skim my celestial honey,
packed into your
crowns of flowers.

I bleed inside you
—the unborn—
webs of this world and the other world,
half-moons,
fleshless fish,
wingless birds,
spineless snakes...
Do not forgive,
sweetheart.

El cazador de paisajes

Levantado
sobre tus dos piernas,
como la torre
en la llanura,
tu cabeza perfecta
cazaba paisajes.

Ya el sol,
último pez del horizonte.
Ya las colinas,
pequeños senos
cubiertos de vello
dorado.

Ya las balumbas
de nubes
heroicas,
ocultadoras
de las trompetas
del trueno,

Sobre la máquina
voladora,
o rodante,
o la torre
de tu cuerpo,
trasponías horizontes
absorbiendo
racimos
de formas
y colores.

Adherida a tu velocidad,
como la hoja
a la rueda,
lancé tímidas flechas
a tus paisajes soberbios.

Y sólo
pequeños
rincones de formas
recogió mi corazón
adormecido.

The Hunter of Landscapes

Raised
on two legs,
like the prairie
tower, your perfect
head hunted
landscapes.

It saw the sun:
last fish of the horizon.
Saw the hills:
small breasts
covered with golden
down.

Saw bundles
of heroic
clouds,
concealers
of thunder's trumpets.

Above the machine
that flies or
rotates
(or the tower
of your body)
you moved horizons,
absorbing
shape and color
clusters.

Attached to your speed,
like a leaf
to a wheel,
I threw timid arrows
at your sublime landscapes.

And my dozing
heart gathered
only small,
shaped corners.

Playa

Parado contra la balaustrada,
de espaldas,
el anciano de sombrero amarillo
está ya muerto.

Le cantan responsos
en ondas monótonas
las masas de agua verde
que me mojan los pies.

Horizonte lejano:
no puedo tocarte.

Las gaviotas sobre mi cabeza
se aman todavía...
Es verdad, pues;
seres vivos se aman todavía:
con alas,
con pies,
con pezuñas,
se aman todavía...

Un niño rubio
ha dicho hoy
en el comedor
con una vocecita
de violoncelo recién regado:
"Mami:
¿puedo comer este durazno?"
Sus palabras
han abierto en gajos
mi corazón.
Por ellas he visto
al hombre muerto de pie,
y el vuelo de las gaviotas,
y el horizonte huidizo.

Beach

Standing with his back
against the balustrade,
the old man with the yellow hat
is already dead.

Monotonous waves
of green water
washing my feet
mourn him with responsories.

Distant horizon,
I cannot touch you.

The gulls on my head
still love one another...
It is true, then,
living beings still love one another;
with wings,
feet,
hooves,
they still love one another...

Today a blond boy
asked in the dining room:
"Mommy,
can I eat this peach?"
His little voice
was a violoncello
recently watered.
The words tore
my heart into pieces.
Because of them I've seen
the man dead on his feet,
the flight of gulls,
the fleeing horizon.

Crepúsculo

El mar inmóvil,
desprendido de sus mandíbulas,
exhala un alma nueva.

No tiene fondo,
buques hundidos,
almas, abrazadas
a sus algas.

Recién nacido,
la cara de Dios,
pálida,
lo mira.

Buques no lo escribieron.
Hombres no lo descifraron,

Peces no lo pudrieron.
Baja a buscarlo
el sol,
precipitándose en llamas
entre bosques violáceos,
y al tocarle la frente
abre puertas de oro
que calan —túneles—
espacios desconocidos.

Escalinatas lentas
descienden al agua
y llegan, desvanecidas,
a mis pies.

Por ellas ascenderé
un día
hasta internarme
más allá del horizonte.

Paredes de agua
me harán cortejo
en la tarde
resplandeciente.

Twilight

Released from its jaws,
the sea—motionless—
exhales a new soul.

Bottomless sea
whose sunken ships
are souls that clasp
the algal weeds.

God's pale face
stares at
the newborn sea.

Ships did not scribe it.
Nor men decipher it.
Neither did fishes rot it.

The searching sun
plunges into flames
of violaceous forests,
and upon touching
the sea's headlands,
it draws open doors
of gold that penetrate
like tunnels into
unknown spaces.

Slow stairways
sink into the water
and arrive, fainted,
at my feet.

I will scale
these one day
until I confine
myself beyond
the horizon.

Walls of water
will woo me
in the resplendent
afternoon.

Agrio está el mundo

Agrio está el mundo,
inmaduro,
detenido;
sus bosques
florecen puntas de acero;
suben las viejas tumbas
a la superficie;
el agua de los mares
acuna
casas de espanto.

Agrio está el sol
sobre el mundo,
ahogado en los vahos
que de él ascienden,
inmaduro,
detenido.

Agria está la luna
sobre el mundo;
verde,
desteñida;
caza fantasmas
con sus patines
húmedos.

Agrio está el viento
sobre el mundo;
alza nubes de insectos muertos,
se ata, roto,
a las torres,
se anuda crespones
de llanto;
pesa sobre los techos.

Agrio está el hombre
sobre el mundo,
balanceándose
sobre sus piernas:

A sus espaldas,
todo,
desierto de piedras;
a su frente,
todo,
desierto de soles,
ciego...

The World Is Sour

The world is sour,
unripe, detained;
its forests
bloom steel points;
the old tombs rise
to the surface;
sea water rocks
houses of fright.

The sun
above the world
is sour, suffocated
by the vapors
that rise from it,
unripe, detained.

The moon
above the world
is sour,
green, discolored;
it hunts ghosts
with humid skates.

The wind
above the world
is sour; it lifts clouds
of dead insects;
broken, it ties itself
to the towers
with weepy crepe knots;
it weighs on rooftops.

The Man
above the world
is sour,
balancing himself
on his legs...

Behind his back
everything
is a stone desert;
in front of him
everything
is a desert of suns,
blinded...

Retrato de García Lorca

Buscando raíces de alas
la frente
se le desplaza
a derecha
a izquierda.

Y sobre el remolino
de la cara
se le fija,
telón del más allá,
comba y ancha.

Una alimaña
le grita en la nariz
que intenta aplastársele
enfurecida...

Irrumpe un griego
por sus ojos distantes.

Un griego
que sofocan de enredaderas
las colinas andaluzas
de sus pómulos
y el valle trémulo
de la boca.

Salta su garganta
hacia fuera
pidiendo
la navaja lunada
de aguas filosas.

Cortádsela.
De norte a sur.
De este a oeste.

Dejad volar la cabeza,
la cabeza sola,
herida de ondas marinas
negras...
Y de guedejones de sátiro
que le caen
como campánulas
en la cara
de máscara antigua.

Apagadle
la voz de madera,
cavernosa,
arrebujada
en las catacumbas nasales.

Libradlo de ella,
y de sus brazos dulces,
y de su cuerpo terroso.

Forzadle sólo,
antes de lanzarlo
al espacio,
el arco de las cejas
hasta hacerlos puentes
del Atlántico,
del Pacífico...

Por donde los ojos,
navíos extraviados,
circulen
sin puertos
ni orillas...

Portrait of García Lorca

Searching for winged roots,
his forehead
shifts
to the right,
to the left.

A curtain of the afterlife
fixes
on the whirlpool
of his wide
and curved face.

A furious pest
screams,
squashing itself
on his nose...

Out of his distant eyes
a Greek bursts out,

whose cheek bones
—Andalusian hills—
whose mouth
—a tremulous valley—
choke him
with climbing plants.

His throat
leaps out
asking for
the half-moon razor
of cutting waters.

Cut it.
From north to south.
From east to west.

Let his head fly,
his head alone,
wounded by black
waves...
satyr shells
falling
like bellflowers
over his face,
an ancient mask.

Turn off
the wooden, cavernous
voice,
muffled
in nasal catacombs.

Free him from it,
and from his sweet arms,
and from his earthy body.

Before launching
him into space,
force together the arch
of his eyebrows
until you've made them
bridges over the Atlantic,
over the Pacific...

So that his eyes,
like stray warships,
can circulate
without ports
or shores....

Retrato de un muchacho que se llama Sigfrido

Tu nombre suena
como los cuernos de caza
despertando las selvas vírgenes.

Y tu nariz aleteante,
triángulo de cera vibrátil,
es la avanzada
de tu beso joven.

Tu piel morena
rezuma
cantos bárbaros.

Pero tu mirada de aguilucho,
abridora simultánea
de siete caminos,
es latina.

Y tu voz,
untada de la humedad del Plata,
ya es criolla.

Te curva las arterias
el agua del Rhin.

El tango
te desarticula
la voluntad.

Y el charleston
te esculpe
el cuerpo.

Tus manos,
heridas de intrincados caminos,
son la historia
de una raza
de amadores.

En tu labio
de sangre huyente
el grito de las valkirias
se estremece todavía.

Tu cuello es un pedúnculo
quebrado por tus sueños.

De tu pequeña cabeza
fina
emergen ciudades heroicas.

No he visto tu corazón:
debe abrirse
en largos pétalos
grises.

He visto tu alma:
lágrima
ensanchada en mar azul:

Al evaporarse
el infinito se puebla
de lentas colinas malva.

Tus piernas
no son las columnas
del canto salomónico:
suavemente se arquean
bajo la cadena de hombres
que te precedió.

Tienes un deseo: morir.
Y una esperanza: no morir.

Portrait of a Boy Named Siegfried

Your name sounds
like hunting horns
waking virgin forests.

And your fluttery nose,
a vibratory wax triangle,
is the reconnoiterer
of your young kiss.

Your swarthy skin
seeps
barbarian songs.

But your eaglet's gaze,
simultaneous opener
of seven roads,
is Latin.

And your voice,
anointed with the Plate's humidity,
is already creole.

The Rhine's water
curves your arteries.

The tango
disjoints
your will.

And the Charleston
sculpts
your body.

Your hands,
wounded with criss-crossing roads,
are the history
of a race
of lovers.

The Valkyries' wild scream
still trembles
in your lip,
its blood fleeing.

Your neck is a peduncle
broken by your dreams.

Heroic cities emerge
from your small
fine head.

I have not seen your heart.
It must open
into large
gray petals.

I have seen your soul:
teardrop that's widened
into a blue sea.

When the infinite
evaporates, it is settled
by slow mauve hills.

Your legs
are not the columns
in Solomon's song:
they arch softly
beneath the chain of men
that preceded you.

You have a wish: to die.
And a hope: not to die.

Llama

Sobre la cruz del tiempo
clavada estoy.
Mi queja abre la pulpa
del corazón divino
y su estremecimiento
aterciopela
el musgo de la tierra.

Un ámbar agridulce
destilado de las
flores cerúleas
cae a mojar
mis labios sedientos.

Ríos de sangre
bajan de mis manos
a salpicar el rostro
de los hombres.
Sobre la cruz del tiempo
clavada estoy.

El rumor lejano
del mundo, ráfaga cálida,
evapora el sudor
de mi frente.

Mis ojos, faros de angustia,
trazan señales misteriosas
en los mares desiertos.
Y eterna,
la llama de mi corazón
sube en espirales
a iluminar el horizonte.

Flame

I am nailed
to the cross of time.
My moaning opens the pulp
of the divine heart,
and its shuddering
turns to velvet
the earth's moss.

A semisweet amber,
distilled from
cerulean flowers,
falls down to wet
my thirsty lips.

Rivers of blood
fall down my hands
to sprinkle
men's faces.
I am nailed
to the cross of time.

The world's
distant murmur—a hot gust—
evaporates the sweat
on my forehead.

My eyes, lighthouses of anguish,
trace mysterious signs
on desert seas.
Eternal,
my heart's flame
rises in spirals
to light up the horizon.

Yo en el fondo del mar

En el fondo del mar
hay una casa
de cristal.

A una avenida
de madréporas,
da.

Un gran pez de oro,
a las cinco,
me viene a saludar.

Me trae
un rojo ramo
de flores de coral.

Duermo en una cama
un poco más azul
que el mar.

Un pulpo
me hace guiños
a través del cristal.

En el bosque verde
que me circunda
—din don... din dan—
se balancean y cantan
las sirenas
De nácar verdemar.

Y sobre mi cabeza
arden, en el crepúsculo,
las erizadas puntas del mar.

I Live on the Sea Floor

There's a glass house
on the sea floor.

On an avenue
of white coral.

A large golden fish
comes to greet me
at five.

It brings
a bouquet of red
coral flowers.

I sleep on a bed
a little bluer
than the sea.

An octopus
winks at me
through the glass.

In the green forest
that surrounds me
—ding dong... ding dang—
mother-of-pearl mermaids,
green as the sea,
poise and sing.

At twilight
bristling crests
burn above my head.

Alta mar

Fantasma negro,
cabeceando en el azul de la noche,
cruz del palo mayor:
vigila.

Tiburones escoltan
el buque
y asoman sus cabezas:
¡llama!

Está solo el cielo,
está solo el mar,
está solo el hombre...
Cruz del palo mayor:
¡grita!

High Seas

Main mast a cross,
the black phantasm
pitches in the blue of night.
It keeps watch.

Sharks escort
the ship
and jut their heads.
It calls out.

The sky is alone,
the sea is alone,
mankind is alone...
Main mast a cross,
the ship shouts.

Nácar marino

Columnas de plata sostienen el cielo;
varas de jacinto se levantan del mar;
trepan a la bóveda
guirnaldas de flores de sal.

Escamas de sirenas de nácar
envuelven las serpientes
espejeantes del mar.

Detrás del firmamento
rueda su bola fría
un sol blanco de cristal.

Su luz esmerilada
llama a todos los peces del mar.

Verticales,
asomando las bocas rosadas,
todos los peces están.

Nacre

Silver columns hold the sky;
hyacinth rods rise from the sea;
garlands of salt flowers
clamber up to the vault.

The nacreous scales
of mermaids wrap
shimmery sea serpents.

Its cold ball—
a white crystal sun—
rolls behind the firmament.

Its emery-polished light
beckons all the sea's fishes.

They appear
vertical,
rosy mouths peeping.

Tormenta y hombres

Elásticos de agua
mecen la casa marina.

Como a tropa
la tiran.

La tapa del cielo
desciende en tormenta ceñida;
su lazo negro
vigila.

Asoman en la tinta del agua
su cabeza estúpida las bestias marinas.

¡Y el ojo humano
se sesga todavía!...

Grupos de hombres, hostiles,
sobre el buque,
se miran...

Storm and Men

Elastic bands of water
rock the sea house.

And knock it down
like troops.

The sky's lid
comes down tight in a storm;
its black ribbon
watches.

The stupid heads of sea beasts
peek out in the inky water.

And the human eye
still slants… !

On the ship
groups of hostile men
watch one another…

Faro en la noche

Esfera negra el cielo
y disco negro el mar.

Abre en la costa, el faro,
su abanico solar.

¿A quién busca en la noche
que gira sin cesar?

Si en el pecho me busca
el corazón mortal,

Mire la roca negra
donde clavado está.

Un cuervo pica siempre,
pero no sangra ya.

Lighthouse in the Night

The sky is a black sphere,
the sea a black disc.

The lighthouse unfurls its solar
fan along the coastline.

For whom does it search in the night
that spins endlessly?

If it searches my breast
for the mortal heart,

Let it look in the black rock
where it is nailed.

A raven always pecks,
but it bleeds no more.

Mañana gris

Se abren bocas grises
en la plancha
redonda del mar.

Tragan nubes grises
las bocas
silenciosas del mar.

Dormidos los peces,
en el fondo,
están.

Colocados en nichos,
el cuerpo frío horizontal,
duermen todos los peces
del mar.

Uno, bajo una aleta,
tiene un pequeño
sol invernal.

Su luz difusa
asciende
y abre una aurora pálida
en cada boca gris del mar.

Pasa el buque
y los peces
no se pueden despertar.

Gaviotas trazan signos de cero
sobre la inmensidad.

Gray Morning

Gray mouths open
in the round
plate of the sea.

The sea's silent
mouths
swallow gray clouds.

The fishes
are asleep
in the bottom.

Placed in niches—
the cold body horizontal—
all the sea's fishes
sleep.

One, beneath its fin,
has a small
wintry sun.

Its diffused light
rises
and opens a pale dawn
in each gray mouth of the sea.

A ship passes
and the fishes
cannot wake up.

Gulls trace zeroes
over the immensity.

Trópico

Cálida, morada, viva,
la carne fría del mar.

Trópico que maduras los frutos:
maduraste el agua con sal;
con terciopelo
ataste las olas
y las has echado
a soñar.

Cálida,
morada,
viva,
la carne fría
del mar.

Para mi carne
que se acaba
tu terciopelo
de coral.

Envuelta en él
como una llama
que se desplaza
sobre el mar,
tallo erguido
en la tarde,
arder,
chisporrotear...

Tropics

Cold flesh
of the sea:
warm, purple, alive,

O Tropics,
ripener of fruits,
you ripened water
with salt,
tied the waves
with velvet
and made them
dream.

Cold flesh
of the sea,
warm,
purple,
alive.

Your coral
of velvet
has died
for my flesh,

my flesh
that dwells
inside
like a seaborne
flame,
burning,
sparking,
stalk-straight
in the afternoon…

Marcha en silencio

La mole negra
del buque, avanza,

Se abren en silencio
los valles de agua.

Ojos fosforescentes
asoman a los pozos de las aguas:
¿Sirenas en hileras,
hacen, acaso, guardia?

Única voz del mar,
una cadena, roe la planchada.

Un fantasma blanco,
sobre el puente, comanda.

Silent March

The black ship
advances:
a behemoth.

Valleys of water
cleave in silence.

Phosphorescent eyes
appear in pools of water.
Do rows of mermaids
perhaps stand guard?

A chain, the sea's only voice,
gnaws the gangplank.

Above the bridge
a white ghost commands.

Vaticinio

Un día,
la ciudad que desde arriba
veo,
se levantará sobre sus flancos
y caminará.
Sus grandes remos
de hierro,
moviéndose a un compás
solemne,
avanzarán río adentro
y el agua
los sostendrá.
Con su ancha proa roma,
hecha para calar
en el horizonte
túneles gigantes,
sus selvas de chimeneas,
lanzas negras;
sus nieblas y sus penachos
y su ejército de casas,
ordenado por una
voluntad prevista,
dejará sus húmedos
sótanos coloniales,
y, atravesando el mar,
entrará en la Tierra
gastada y luminosa
de los Hombres.

Prophecy

The city that I see
from above
will one day
rise
on its flanks
and walk.
Its great iron
oars,
rowing to a solemn
rhythm,
will move deep
into the river,
and the waters
will support
them.

Its prow—
wide, blunt—
has been
fashioned
to gouge
huge tunnels
in the horizon.

City of clouds
and fog tufts
whose chimneys
are a jungle
of black spears,

whose army
of houses
(commanded by
a power foretold)
will leave its musty
colonial basements
and, crossing the sea,
enter the wasted
and luminous Earth
of Humankind.

Calle

Un callejón abierto
entre altos paredones grises.
A cada momento
la boca oscura de las puertas,
los tubos de los zaguanes,
trampas conductoras
a las catacumbas humanas.
¿No hay un escalofrío
en los zaguanes?
¿Un poco de terror
en la blancura ascendente
de una escalera?
Paso con premura.
Todo ojo que me mira
me multiplica y dispersa
por la ciudad.
Un bosque de piernas,
Un torbellino de círculos
rodantes,
una nube de gritos y ruidos,
me separan la cabeza del tronco,
las manos de los brazos,
el corazón del pecho,
los pies del cuerpo,
la voluntad de su engarce.
Arriba
el cielo azul
aquieta su agua transparente:
ciudades de oro
lo navegan.

Street

An alley gapes
between high gray walls.
At every moment
the door's black mouth
and the lobby's pipes
are traps that lead
to the human catacombs.
Is there no shivering
in the lobbies?
A bit of terror
in the ascending whiteness
of a stairway?
I walk with haste.
Every roving eye
multiplies and scatters me
throughout the city.
A forest of legs,
a whirlwind
of rolling circles,
and a cloud of screams
and noises sever
my head from the torso,
hands from arms,
heart from breast,
legs from the body,
the will from its mounting.
The blue sky
above
calms its transparent water,
which golden cities
navigate.

Selvas de ciudad

En semicírculo
se abre
la selva de casas:
unas al lado de otras,
unas detrás de otras,
unas encima de otras,
unas delante de otras,
todas lejos de todas.
Moles grises que caminan
hasta que los brazos
se le secan
en el aire frío del sur.
Moles grises que se multiplican
hasta que la bocanada
de horno del norte
les afloja las articulaciones.
Siempre hacienda el signo
de la cruz.
Reproduciéndose por ángulos.
Con las mismas ventanas
de juguetería.
Las mismas azoteas rojizas.
Las mismas cúpulas pardas.
Los mismos frentes desteñidos.
Las mismas rejas sombrías.
Los mismos buzones rojos.
Las mismas columnas negras.
Los mismos focos amarillos.
Debajo de los techos,
otra selva,
una selva humana,
debe moverse
pero no en línea recta.
Troncos extraños,
de luminosas copas,
se agitan indudablemente

movidos por un viento
que no silba.
Pero no alcanzo sus actitudes,
ni oigo sus palabras,
ni veo el resplandor
de sus ojos.
Son muy anchas las paredes;
muy espesos los techos.

City Jungles

The jungle of houses
opens up
in a half-circle:
some next to others,
some behind others,
some on top of others,
some in front of others,
but all apart.
Gray hulks that walk
until their arms
dry up
in the cold air of the south.
Gray hulks that multiply
until the oven-like puffs
of the north
loosen their joints.
Always making the sign
of the cross.
Reproducing themselves
by angles.
With the same toyshop
windows.
The same reddish flat roofs.
The same brown copulas.
The same discolored façades.
The same gloomy grates.
The same red mailboxes.
The same black columns.
The same yellow light bulbs.
Below the roofs
must move,
though not in a straight line,
another jungle,
a human jungle.
Strange trunks

with luminous tops
stir, moved no doubt
by a wind
that doesn't whistle.
But I don't grasp their attitudes,
nor hear their words,
nor see the gleem of their eyes.
The walls are very wide,
the roofs very thick.

Hombres en la ciudad

Arden los bosques
del horizonte;
esquivando llamas,
cruzan, veloces,
los gamos azules
del crepúsculo.

Cabritos de oro
emigran hacia
la bóveda
y se recuestan
en los musgos azules.

Se alza
debajo,
enorme,
la rosa de cemento,
la ciudad,
inmóvil en su tronco
de sótanos sombríos.

Emergen
—cúpulas, torres—
sus negros pistilos
a la espera del polen
lunar.

Ahogados
por las llamas de la hoguera,
y perdidos
entre los pétalos
de la rosa,
invisibles casi,
de un lado a otro,
los hombres...

Men in the City

Forests of the horizon
are burning;
twilight's blue deer
cross swiftly,
swerving the flames.

Golden kids
emigrate to
the sky's vault
and lie on
blue mosses.

The enormous rose
of cement
rises from below,
the city motionless
in its trunk
of somber basements.

Domes and towers
emerge,
their black pistils
awaiting lunar
pollen.

Choked
by the bonfire's
flames, lost among
the rose's petals,
the men amble
from place to place,
almost invisible.

Llovizna

Descoloridas, heladas,
las casas
—nichos en hilera—
se aprietan unas
contra otras.
El sol
juega
en jardines
lejanos;
sus pasos distantes
entristecen
la bóveda.

No logran hallarlo
los penachos de humo:
tumbados al nacer
se abrazan a las cruces
y traban las cúpulas.

Había un río a orilla
de la ciudad...
se ha echado a andar
también,
mar adentro,
con pies
de felpa.

¿O lo ha tragado, lento,
el bostezo neblinoso
de la tarde?...

Planchadas
contra el horizonte
están las chimeneas:
sus horquillas cazan
con displicencia
las alas de ángeles mohínos
que, a grandes zancadas,
rozan las cornisas.

Una cinta de luz
lechosa
ata la cintura
de la ciudad:
las puntas desflecadas
del lazo
latiguean la bóveda
hasta que el polvo de agua
las empapa
y tumba.

Drizzle

Discolored, frozen,
the houses
—niches in a row—
squeeze against
each other.
The sun
plays
in distant
gardens;
its distant steps
sadden
the sky's vault.

Tufts of smoke
fail to find the sun;
prostrate at birth,
they hug crosses
and knot cupolas.

There was once a river
on the city's edge…
it also has flowed
toward the open sea
with felt feet.

Or has the misty yawn
of afternoons
slowly swallowed it?…

Chimneys
are pressed
against the horizon:
their pitchforks
hunt in vain
wings of sad angels
who, striding,
graze cornices.

A strip
of milky light
ties the city's waist:
the ribbon's
frayed edges
whip the vault
until the watery powder
drenches
and tumbles them.

Mascarilla y trébol
Mask and Clover
(1938)

A Eros

He aquí que te cacé por el pescuezo
a la orilla del mar, mientras movías
las flechas de tu aljaba para herirme
y vi en el suelo tu floreal corona.

Como a un muñeco destripé tu vientre
y examiné sus ruedas engañosas
y muy envuelta en sus poleas de oro
hallé una trampa que decía: sexo.

Sobre la playa, ya un guiñapo triste,
te mostré al sol, buscón de tus hazañas,
ante un corro asustado de sirenas.

Iba subiendo por la cuesta albina
tu madrina de engaños, Doña Luna,
y te arrojé a la boca de las olas.

To Eros

This is the seashore where I caught you
by the neck, while you picked arrows
from your quiver to wound me. I saw
on the ground your crown of flowers.

I disemboweled you like a doll
and examined your belly's deceitful
wheels. I found well wrapped
in its gold pulleys a trap that said: sex.

You were already a sad rag on the beach.
I held you up to the sun, searcher of your deeds,
in view of a frightened ring of sirens.

Your godmother of deceits, Doña Luna,
was climbing the albinic slope,
and I tossed you into the mouth of waves.

Río de La Plata en negro y ocre

La niebla había comido su horizonte
y sus altas columnas agrisadas
se echaban hacia el mar y parapetos
eran sobre la atlántica marea.

Se estaba anclado allí, ferruginoso,
viendo venir sus padres desde el norte;
dos pumas verdes que por monte y piedra
saltaban desde el trópico a roerlo:

Porque ni bien nacido ya moría
y en su desdén apenas se rizaba
señor de sí, los labios apretados.

Lavadas rosas le soltaba el cielo
y de su seno erguía tallos de humo
sobre quemados cabeceantes buques.

River Plate in Black and Ocher

The fog had eaten away its horizon,
and its high gray columns leaned
toward the sea, becoming parapets
in the Atlantic tide.

Seeing its parents arrive from the north,
it anchored there, the color of rust;
two green pumas that leapt in copse and rock
came from the tropics to gnaw it:

Though unborn, it was already dying,
and in its scorn it hardly rippled
with self-possession, lips pressed tight.

The sky dropped on it washed-out roses,
and from its breast it lifted stalks
of smoke over burnt and pitching ships.

Río de La Plata en lluvia

Ya casi el cielo te apretaba, ciego,
y sumergida una ciudad tenías
en tu cuerpo de grises heliotropos
neblivelado en su copón de llanto.

Unas lejanas cúpulas tiznaba
tu gran naufragio sobre el horizonte
que la muerta ciudad bajo las ondas
se alzaba a ver el desabrido cielo:

Caía a plomo una llovizna tierna
sobre las pardas cruces desafiantes
en el pluvioso mar desperfiladas.

Y las aves, los árboles, los hombres
dormir querían tu afelpado sueño
liláceo y triste de llanura fría.

River Plate in the Rain

The sky had almost squeezed you,
blind river, while a city lay submerged
inside your body of gray heliotropes,
freeze-misted in its ciborium of sobs.

Your great shipwreck along the horizon
blackened faraway domes,
and the dead city beneath the waves
rose up to watch the dull sky.

A fresh drizzle pounded like lead
those dun, defiant crosses
turned slovenly by the rainy sea.

And birds, trees, men wished to fall
asleep and have your dream—
lilacs' velvet, sad like cold plains.

Danzón porteño

Una tarde, borracha de tus uvas
amarillas de muerte, Buenos Aires,
que alzas en sol de otoño en las laderas
enfriadas del oeste, en los tramontos,

vi plegarse tu negro Puente Alsina
como un gran bandoneón y a sus compases
danzar tu tango entre haraposas luces
a las barcazas rotas del Riachuelo:

Sus venenosas aguas, viboreando
hilos de sangre; y la hacinada cueva;
y los bloques de fábricas mohosas,

echando alientos, por las chimeneas,
de pechos devorados, machacaban
contorsionados su obsedido llanto.

Buenos Aires Danzón

Buenos Aires, you rise in the autumn sun
over western hillsides cooled by northerlies.
Drunk one afternoon on your yellow
grapes of death, I saw your black bridge—

Puente Alsina—fold into the bellows
of a grand accordion, and to its beat
broken river barges danced your danzón
among ragged lights on the poisonous

Riachuelo, its snaking currents
shedding filaments of blood along
the cluttered cellars. Blocks of moldy

factories, smokestacks spewing breath
from lungs devoured, contorted,
pounding their obsessive wail.

Sol de América

Cerrada está mi alcoba y yo viajando
por las playas del sueño donde pesco
antiguos mitos y alza una madrépora
su alma futura que escribirá libros.

(El hombre, la cabeza desmedida,
salta en los pararrayos pero añora
su limo blando donde el alma holgada
dejaba hacer al animal primero.)

Por su canal estrecho la mirilla
dejó filtrar minúscula una mano
del sol ardiente que sacude el sueño.

Crecido está de luces por su llama
mi cuarto oscuro y golpeando afuera
en su cristal de fuego el Nuevo Mundo.

América's Sun

My bedroom shut, and I traveling
in dreamful beaches where I fish
for ancient myths, and a coral reef raises
its future soul that will write books.

(The man, his head disproportionate,
leaps on lightning rods but yearns
for his soft mud where the snug soul
allowed the animal to be made first.)

Through its narrow channel,
the peephole filtered the burning sun's
miniscule hand that shakes the dream.

Aflame, my dark bedroom has grown
immense with light, and knocking outside
its window of fire is the New World.

Ruego a Prometeo

Agrándame tu roca, Prometeo;
entrégala al dentado de la muela
que tritura los astros de la noche
y hazme rodar en ella, encadenada.

Vuelve a encender las furias vengadoras
de Zeus y dame látigo de rayos
contra la boca rota, mas guardando
su ramo de verdad entre los dientes.

Cubre el rostro de Zeus con las gorgonas;
a sus perros azuza y los hocicos
eriza en sus sombríos hipogeos:

He aquí a mi cuerpo como un joven potro
piafante y con la espuma reventada
salpicando las barbas del Olimpo.

Plea to Prometheus

Enlarge your rock for me, Prometheus;
offer it as a tooth to the stone
that grinds night's celestial bodies;
and make me roll in it, chained.

Light again the vengeful Furies
of Zeus and whip me with lightning
bolts against the broken mouth, but preserve
the branch of truth between the teeth.

Cover Zeus's face with the Gorgons,
rouse his hounds, and bristle
the muzzles in their somber hypogea:

My body's like a rearing young colt
whose foam, bursting,
spatters the beards of Olympus.

Tiempo de esterilidad

A la Mujer los números miraron
y dejáronle un cofre en su regazo:
y vio salir de aquél un río rojo
que daba vuelta en espiral al mundo.

Extraños signos, casi indescifrables,
sombreaban sus riberas, y la luna
siniestramente dibujada en ellos,
ordenaba los tiempos de marea.

Por sus crecidas, Ella fue creadora
y los números fríos revelados
en tibias caras de espantados ojos.

Un día de su seno huyóse el río
y su isla verde florecida de hombres
quedó desierta y vio crecer el viento.

Time of Sterility

The numbers looked at the woman
and left a coffer on her lap.
She saw a red river come out
that spiraled around the world.

Strange signs, almost indecipherable,
shadowed their shores, and the moon,
sinisterly drawn within them,
ordained the rise and fall of the tide.

She turned creator by the surging waters,
and the cold numbers revealed themselves
in lukewarm faces, horror-stricken eyes.

One day the river fled from her womb.
Its green island flowering with men
was left deserted, and she saw the wind grow.

Autorretrato barroco

Una máscara griega, enmohecida
en las romanas catacumbas, vino
cortando espacio a mi calzante cara.
El cráneo un viejo mármol carcajeante.

El Nuevo Continente sopló rachas
de trópico y de sud y abrió sus soles
sobre la testa que cambió su acanto
en acerados bucles combativos.

En un cuerpo de luna, tan ligero
que acunaban las rosas tropicales,
un órgano, tremendo de ternura,

me dobló el pecho. Mas, ¿por qué sus sones
contra el cráneo se helaban y expandían
por la burlesca boca acartonada?

Baroque Self-Portrait

Moldy from Roman catacombs,
a Greek mask, flying through space,
fastened to my face, taut as leather.
The skull was old, cackling marble.

The New Contintent blew tropical
gusts from the south, releasing suns
to shine on the head, its acanthus waves
transformed to feisty ringlets of wax.

Inside a body of moonstone, so light
that tropical roses were cradled,
an organ of tremendous tenderness

bent my breast. But why did its pealing
sounds, against the skull, freeze then expand
on the wizened mouth of mockery?

La sirena

Llévate el torbellino de las horas
y el cobalto del cielo y el ropaje
de mi árbol de septiembre y la mirada
del que me abría soles en el pecho.

Apágame las rosas de la cara
y espántame la risa de los labios
y mezquíname el pan entre los dientes,
vida; y el ramo de mis versos, niega.

Mas déjame la máquina de azules
que suelta sus poleas en la frente
y un pensamiento vivo entre las ruinas;

Lo haré alentar como sirena en campo
de mutilados y las rotas nubes
por él se harán al cielo, vela en alto.

Siren

Take away time's whirlwind,
sky's cobalt, the garments
of my September tree, the gaze
of he who opened suns in my chest.

Extinguish the roses on my face,
shoo the laughter in my lips,
eat away the bread of life between
my teeth; deny the branch of my verses.

But leave me the machine of blue colors
that frees its pulleys in my forehead
and a vivid thought among the ruins;

I will raise its hopes like a siren
in a field of mutilated beings, and by its power
broken clouds will go to heaven, sails raised.

Ultrateléfono

¿Con Horacio? — Ya sé que en la vejiga
tienes ahora un nido de palomas
y tu motocicleta de cristales
vuela sin hacer ruido por el cielo.

—¿Papá? —He soñado que tu damajuana
está crecida como el Tupungato;
aún contiene tu cólera y mis versos.
Echa una gota. Gracias. Ya estoy buena.

Iré a veros muy pronto; recibidme
con aquel sapo que maté en la quinta
de San Juan ¡pobre sapo! y a pedradas.

Miraba como buey y mis dos primos
lo remataron; luego con sartenes
funeral tuvo; y rosas lo seguían.

Phone Call to the Afterlife

Speaking to Horacio? "I already know
that in your bladder you now have a nest
of doves, that your glass motorcycle
flies through heaven noiselessly."

Papá? "I dreamt that your demijohn
had grown like the Tupungato;
it still holds your rage and my poems.
Spill a drop. Thanks. I'm well now."

I will visit you very soon; greet me
with that toad I killed in the villa of San Juan.
Poor toad! And with stones, no less.

He watched like an ox as my two cousins
finished him off; later on he had a funeral
with frying pans and a cortege of roses.

Cigarra en noche de luna

Atalayada, agita la matraca
de su voz, que traspasa el horizonte
del árbol, la cigarra, y llama a mitin
a los grillos en camas de rocío.

Sobre los tanques frescos de los sapos
los grillos mueven verdes batallones.
Manda la capitana chilladora
y cercan los balcones de la luna.

Con peluca de nieve, la levita
de Orion abotonada, y muy de azules,
una mano de azufre, otra de yeso,

la luna dobla el cuerpo saludando;
y los grillos levantan, bayonetas,
hacia su reina las agudas patas.

Cicada in a Moonlit Night

Ensconced in its watchtower,
the cicada's rattle pierces the horizon
of trees. It rallies forth the crickets
that lie on beds of dew.

The crickets field green battalions
against the freshwater tanks of toads.
The female captain screeches commands,
and they encircle the moon's balconies.

Wearing a snow wig and a buttoned-up
frock coat of Orion, intensely blue,
the moon bends its body as it salutes

with one hand of sulfur, the other plaster.
And the crickets lift up to their queen
their sharp legs, bayonets.

Jardín zoológico de nubes

Quiero cantar al que se mueve arriba:
salud, osito tierno, tu señora
se besa con el otro algodonada
y cuando el diente clavas, se deshace.

Y la serpiente que me perseguía
en los sueños, está; y hay una garza
rosada que se viene desde el río
y la ballena destripada llora.

Y está el gato listado que una mano
mató porque era grande y poco pulcro
y en el tejado escándalos alzaba.

Y mi perro lanudo que se sienta
en las traseras patas y se expande
en un castillo que trastorna al viento.

Zoo of Clouds

I want to sing to the one that moves above:
cheers, tender teddy bear, your cottony
mistress kisses the other one and when
you sink your teeth, she comes apart.

And the snake that chased me
in dreams remains; and there is a pink
crane that comes from the river
and the disemboweled whale cries.

And here too is the tabby that some
hand killed because it was big, unclean,
and on the rooftop it raised a ruckus.

And my hairy dog that sits
on its hind legs expands itself
into a castle that vexes the wind.

El cielo

Casas destartaladas las estrellas;
en sus camas, sin sábanas, alumbrando
el ronco animal hembra y los desnudos
sexos al sol picados y rapaces.

Y la boca del ser abierta toda
para tragar los mares de la muerte
y las guerras saltando por los techos
del solar habitado del espacio.

¡Ay!, qué poeta inmenso abrió el torrente
del engaño, que pudo darme el cielo
—atroz de llanto y de miseria—alzado

en un jardín de flores diminutas,
como niños que juegan, con su antorcha,
a no toparse en el azul camino!

The Sky

Stars are disheveled houses.
In their beds without sheets they light up
the hoarse she-animal and the naked sexes—
rapacious and sun-scorched.

The creature's mouth is wide open
for swallowing death's seas.
Warfare jumps from roof to roof
in the occupied lots of space.

Which colossal poet opened deceit's
torrent? Who could have given me a sky
made dreadful from cries and misery?

A sky tossed up in a garden of tiny flowers,
as if children were playing with its torch
a game of hide-and-seek on the blue road.

El sueño

Máscara tibia de otra más helada
sobre tu cara cae y si te borra
naces para un paisaje de neblina
en que tus muertos crecen, la flor corre.

Allí el mito despliega sus arañas;
y enflora la sospecha; y se deshace
la cólera de ayer y el iris luce;
y alguien que ya no es más besa tu boca;

Que un no ser, que es un más ser, doblado,
prendido estás aquí y estás ausente
por praderas de magias y de olvido.

¿Qué alentador sagaz, tras el reposo,
creó este renacer de la mañana
que es juventud del día volvedora?

The Dream

Over your face falls the lukewarm
version of a frozen mask, and if erased,
you'd be born into a landscape of fog
where your dead grow and the flower droops.

It's a place where myth unfolds its spiders
and suspicion blossoms; yesterday's rage
breaks apart and the iris scintillates; and someone
who has ceased to be kisses your mouth.

The state of being is greater than nonbeing—
you are here bent, clutching; you are absent
in the prairies of magic and oblivion.

After the repose, what shrewd encouragement
caused this morning to be reborn,
this youth of a new day?

Un lápiz

Por diez centavos lo compré en la esquina
y vendiómelo un ángel desgarbado;
cuando a sacarle punta lo ponía
lo vi como un cañón pequeño y fuerte.

Saltó la mina que estallaba ideas
y otra vez despuntólo el ángel triste.
Salí con él y un rostro de alto bronce
lo arrió de mi memoria. Distraída

lo eché en el bolso entre pañuelos, cartas,
resecas flores, tubos colorantes,
billetes, papeletas y turrones.

Iba hacia no sé dónde y con violencia
me alzó cualquier vehículo, y golpeando
iba mi bolso con su bomba adentro.

A Pencil

I bought it at the corner for ten cents,
sold to me by a gawky angel.
When I was sharpening it, I saw
it like a small and powerful cannon.

The lead bursting with ideas chipped,
and again the sad angel sharpened the point.
I left with it, and a high-bronze face
carted it from my memory. Distracted,

I threw it in the purse, along with handkerchiefs,
letters, desiccated flowers, lipsticks,
tickets, slips of paper, and nougat candy.

Where I was going I couldn't tell. A vehicle
lifted me with violence, and my purse
went along pounding with its bomb.

A Madona poesía

Aquí a tus pies lanzada, pecadora,
contra tu tierra azul, mi cara oscura,
tú, virgen entre ejércitos de palmas
que no encanecen como los humanos.

No me atrevo a mirar tus ojos puros
ni a tocarte la mano milagrosa:
miro hacia atrás y un río de lujurias
me ladra contra ti, sin culpa alzada.

Una pequeña rama verdecida
en tu orla pongo con humilde intento
de pecar menos, por tu fina gracia,

ya que vivir cortada de tu sombra
posible no me fue, que me cegaste
cuando nacida con tus hierros bravos.

To the Madonna of Poetry

I, sinner, throw myself at your feet,
my dark face against your blue earth.
You, virgin among armies of palms
that do not gray like human beings.

I do not dare gaze at your pure eyes
nor touch your miraculous hand.
I look back and a river of lechery
barks against you, even if blameless.

With humble intent to sin less (may
your purity grace me), I offer this small
branch that greened again in your orle.

I could never live without your shadow,
for you blinded me the day I was brought
to life with your fierce iron forceps.

Uncollected Poems

Un tranvía

Sobre dos vías de luna
se mueve
el feo animal
de hierro y madera.
Su cara cuadrada y hosca
se agranda al acercarse.
Sus fríos ojos
de colores,
y la cifra
de su frente
nos recuerdan un barrio
donde hemos vivido.
Monótona y antipática,
su voz metálica
nos invita a aceptar
el destino.

Streetcar

The ugly animal
of iron and wood
moves
on two moon rails.
Square-faced and surly,
it grows bigger
as it approaches.
Its cold, colored eyes
and the number
on its forehead
remind us of a neighborhood
in which we've lived.
Monotonous and shrill,
its metallic voice
invites us to accept
our destiny.

Niebla

La ciudad está enterrada
bajo la niebla.
Quejas largas,
quejas que vienen
del puerto
atraviesan el aire denso,
filtran los ladrillos,
buscan el camino de mis oídos
y muerden la carne
de mi corazón.
Y son aullidos de terror,
largos, desmayantes,
insistentes:
¿Han visto,
han vista acaso
la cara de un ahogado
flotar sobre las aguas?

Fog

The city is buried
under the fog.
Long-winded gripes
from the seaport
cross the dense air,
seep into the bricks,
search my ears' road,
and bite the flesh
of my heart.
They are moans of terror,
long, faintish,
insistent:
Have you seen,
have you perhaps
seen the face
of a drowned man
float in the water?

Nubes y velas

Viene del río,
el cuello estirado,
las alas en cruz,
el pico anhelante,
una garza monstruosa:
las puntas de sus alas rosadas
prenden los extremos del río;
su cuello, plumón de oro,
tira rayas negras
sobre el acero violáceo
del agua.
Su pico, cuchillo de nácar,
va a ensartar
los puentes negros de la Boca.
Debajo de su toldo
de ensueño
los veleros,
enormes mariposas blancas,
muerden vertiginosamente
la plancha
del río.

Clouds and Sails

It comes from the river,
neck stretched,
wings flaring like a cross,
bill eager —
a monstrous crane!
The tips of rosy wings
grasp the river's extremes;
its neck, a golden plume,
casts black lines
over the water's violet
steel.
Its bill, a nacreous knife,
will impale
the black bridges of the Boca.
Beneath their awning
of dreams,
sailboats —
enormous white butterflies —
bite vertiginously
the river's plating.

Otoño

Pinceles enloquecidos
han tintado de oro
la ciudad.
En el semicírculo
que el ojo horada
no hay más que ríos áureos
corriendo sobre las paredes.
¿O son hongos, hongos amarillos,
prietos, minúsculos,
nacidos con violencia de la piedra,
al llamado de una lluvia incolora
que cae y no moja?
El aire frío de mayo,
agua de aquella cálida pintura,
zigzaguea sobre los techos
para licuarla.
El alma, suspensa
entre una y otro, quisiera
envolverse en el manto tibio,
beber el agua fría
maravillosa.

Autumn

Maddened brushes
have tinted
the city gold.
Inside the eye-bored
semicircles,
only golden rivers
run on the walls.
Or are they mushrooms, yellow mushrooms,
dark, miniscule,
born violently from the stone,
called forth by the colorless
rain that falls and doesn't wet?
In the cold air of May,
water from that balmy painting
zigzags over the roofs
to liquefy the city.
The soul, suspended
between two lovers,
wishes to wrap itself inside
the lukewarm mantle,
drink the cold, marvelous
water.

A Horacio Quiroga

Morir como tú, Horacio, en tus cabales,
y así como en tus cuentos, no está mal;
un rayo a tiempo y se acabó la feria…
Allá dirán.

No se vive en la selva impunemente,
ni cara al Paraná.
Bien por tu mano firme, gran Horacio…
Allá dirán.

"Nos hiere cada hora—queda escrito—
nos mata la final."
Unos minutos menos… ¿quién te acusa?
Allá dirán.

Más pudre el miedo, Horacio, que la muerte
que a las espaldas va.
Bebiste bien, que luego sonreías…
Allá dirán.

Sé que la mano obrera te estrecharon,
mas no, si, Alguno, o simplemente Pan,
que no es de fuertes renegar de su obra…
(Más que tú mismo es fuerte quien dirá.)

To Horacio Quiroga

To die like you, Horacio, sound of mind,
like one of your characters, is not at all bad;
a lightning bolt at the right time, and the party's over...
Let them talk.

One does not live in the jungle, nor facing
the Paraná River, with impunity.
Well done by your firm hand, great Horacio.
Let them talk.

"Every hour wounds us—it is written—
the last one kills us. "
A few minutes less... who can blame you?
Let them talk.

Fear rots us more, Horacio, than death
on our backs.
You drank well, for you smiled later on...
Let them talk.

I know that you shook the worker's hand,
whether just Someone's, or simply Pan's.
The strong should not grumble about his labor...
(Gossip is stronger than you.)

Sapo y mar

Azul plomizo
el mar
tejía auroras
amarillas en el confín.

Y un sapo
sobre su voz
crepuscular, dejaba
caer el goterón
metálico
de su habla.

Abierto
el infinito
a mi derecha;
a izquierda
el punto matemático
rompiendo
en un verde
de musgos
oxidados.

Sola. Dispersa.
Una cortina
helada
daba el sí… no…
del pensamiento
huyente.

Y una taza de té
frente a mis ojos
era el único lazo
que me unía,
animal triste,
a mi mortal cadena.

Toad and Sea

Leaden blue,
the sea wove
yellow dawns
in the horizon.

Twilight-voiced,
a toad rained
down the huge
metallic drops
of its speech.

Infinity
lay open
to my right;
and leftward
the mathemical
point that pierced
the greenness
of rusted mosses.

Alone, spread out,
a frozen
curtain conveyed
the yes... no...
of fleeting
thought.

And before my eyes,
I the sad animal,
there was a cup of tea,
the sole bond
to my mortal coil.

Voy a dormir

Dientes de flores, cofia de rocío,
manos de hierbas, tú, nodriza fina,
tenme prestas las sábanas terrosas
y el edredón de musgos encardados.

Voy a dormir, nodriza mía, acuéstame.
Ponme una lámpara a la cabecera,
una constelación, la que te guste:
todas son buenas; bájala un poquito.

Déjame sola: oyes romper los brotes...
te acuna un pie celeste desde arriba
y un pájaro te traza unos compases

para que olvides... Gracias. Ah, un encargo:
si él llama nuevamente por teléfono
le dices que no insista, que he salido...

I'm Going to Sleep

Teeth of flowers, dewy coif,
herbal hands, you, delicate wet-nurse,
have ready for me the earthy sheets
and the quilt of carded moss.

I'm going to sleep, my wet-nurse, put me to bed.
Put a lamp by the headboard,
a constellation, the one you like;
all are good; lower it just a bit.

Leave me alone; you hear plants sprouting...
from on high a celestial foot rocks you
and a bird traces musical bars in flight

so that you'll forget... Thanks.
Ah, a request: if he phones again
tell him not to insist, that I've gone out...

Notes

[1] "la franqueza de 'la señorita Alfonsina Storni' quien, a contramanos de las costumbres de la época seguidas por la mayoría de las mujeres, se atrave a tomar la palabra y a expresar públicamente sus deseos, sus sentimientos y sus ideas."

[2] In Latin America and in Spain, the term *modernismo* denotes more of an association with the French Symbolists and Parnassians than to the Modernism of T.S. Eliot and Ezra Pound.

[3] "Alfonsina se ha mostrado 'egoista, burlona y alguna vez voluntariamente banal'."

[4] "Horacio Quiroga pertenece al grupo de los instintivos geniales, de los escritores desiguales, arbitrarios, unilaterales y personalísimos."

[5] "... yo he debido vivir como un varón; yo reclamo para mí una moral de varón."

[6] "Me repugna la gente feliz. La felicidad me parece el más perfecto estado de animalidad."

[7] "fuertes arrebatos de inspiración."

[8] "Alfonsina pasa de manera sorpresiva del llanto a la risa, de la tristeza a la alegría."

[9] "un desplazamiento estético, la búsqueda de renovación...que combine el apego a las formas conocidas con poemas concebidos desde lo anticonvencional y rupturista."

[10] "sobre el suave vaivén entre el concepto y la palabra, entre lo universal y lo personal."

[11] "I will throw myself into the sea."

[12] "mis mejores composiciones las he producido en los momentos de angustia y de dolor."

[13] "me han brotado vitalmente en contenido y forma, casi en estado de trance (el empuje inicial de la idea creó de por sí la manera suelta) ya que escribí la mayoría en pocos minutos...aunque cepillarlos me haya demandado meses."

[14] "colaboración imaginativa."

[15] "hondo escepticismo...agotamiento espiritual...desencanto con el mundo."

Works Cited

Delgado, Josefina. *Alfonsina Storni: una biografía*. Second edition. Buenos Aires: Planeta, 1991.

Galán, Silvia and Graciela Gliemmo. *La otra Alfonsina*. Buenos Aires: Aguilar, 2002.

Jones, Sonia. *Alfonsina Storni*. Boston: Twayne, 1979.

Kirkpatrick, Gwen. "Alfonsina Storni (29 May 1892 - 25 October 1938)." *Modern Spanish American Poets*, *First Series*. Ed. María A. Salgado. Detroit, MI: Gale, 2003, 336-344.

Storni, Alfonsina. *Obras*. Volume I. Ed. Delfina Muschietti. Buenos Aires: Losada, 1999.